DYNAMIC COVER LETTERS

*How to sell yourself to an employer
by writing a letter
that will get your resume read,
get you an interview
and get you a job!*

*by Katharine Hansen
with Randall S. Hansen*

Ten Speed Press
Berkeley, California

1🔄

Ten Speed Press
Box 7123
Berkeley, California 94707

Cover design by Fifth Street Design
Text design by Hal Hershey
Illustrations on pages 2 and 3 by Ellen Sasaki
Handwriting by Cindy Cappa

Library of Congress Cataloging-in-Publication Data
Hansen, Katharine
    Dynamic cover letters : how to sell yourself
to an employer by writing a letter that will
get your resume read, get you an interview—
and get you a job! / by Katharine Hansen
with Randall S. Hansen.
      p. cm.
  ISBN 0-89815-356-5 : $6.95
  1. Cover letters.   2. Resumes (Employ
  ment)   I. Hansen, Randall S.   II, Title.
HF5383.H28 190
650.14—dc20   89-77576
                             CIP

Printed in the United States of America

6 7 8 9 10 — 95 94 93 92

TO THREE SPECIAL MEN:

To my father, William Dayton Sumner, for inspiring me to write;

To my uncle, John N. Sumner, for nurturing my writing;

*To my Latin teacher, David L. Rhody, who inspired
a love of words and learning*

Contents

Introduction

Lots of books are written about resumes, and many of them even have a short chapter on cover letters. I believe the importance of cover letters has been vastly underplayed.

After all, it *is* the first thing a prospective employer sees when you send in your resume.

Experts on job-hunting say that your resume is not supposed to get you a job; it gets you an interview. But the only way you're going to get an interview is if your resume is read.

The best way to ensure it will be read is to write a dynamic cover letter, one that will arouse the potential employer's interest. This book will show you how to write that dynamic cover letter.

What qualifies me to write about cover letters? I'm not a career counselor. My training has come from the trenches of job-hunting. I've used cover letters successfully in a number of job searches. Here are some stats from a recent job search:

Out of 218 cover letters with resumes that I sent out in response to help wanted ads only (rather than to cold contacts), I heard from 75 employers. Of these 75:

- ❏ 37 prospective employers interviewed me
- ❏ 14 prospective employers called me to invite me for an interview, but I declined for reasons such as the positions paid too little or were too far away
- ❏ 11 prospective employers sent rejection letters without interviewing me

- ❏ 2 prospective employers offered me jobs that I declined
- ❏ 1 employer offered me a job I accepted.

For every 5.9 cover letters with resumes I sent, I got an interview.

For every 4.3 cover letters with resumes I sent, I got an invitation for an interview.

Considering that the experts say only one resume in 245 results in an interview, I give my cover letters a lot of credit in helping me get interviews.

My resume mailing produced a response rate of almost 25 percent. In direct-mail marketing, a 1 percent response rate is considered very good. Again, I credit my letters with improving my odds.

I've also been in the position to hire employees. Hundreds of cover letters—from the terrific to the atrocious—have come across my desk (and many of them, with name and other identifying features changed to protect the writer's privacy, appear in the sample section of this book.) I can speak from an employer's perspective; I know what turns employers on and what makes them toss your letter right in the circular file.

Finally, I'm a writer and editor, so I believe I am able to apply my craft to the art of writing dynamic cover letters. With this book, I hope to help you to write dynamic cover letters that will prompt employers to call you for interviews.

—*Katharine Hansen*

Send Not Thy Resume
Naked into the World

What is a cover letter? Also known as a letter of introduction, letter of application, transmittal letter, or broadcast letter, it's a letter that no smart job-seeker should send his or her resume without. Few employers seriously consider a resume that is not accompanied by a cover letter. I know I didn't when I was in a hiring position.

Why is a cover letter so important? A resume is useless to an employer if he or she doesn't know what kind of work you want to do. A cover letter tells them the type of position you're seeking.

A dynamic cover letter can give you an edge in the competitive world of job-hunting. The experts say that only two to five of every hundred resumes survive the screening process. Clearly, you can increase your chances of being invited for an interview by writing an effective cover letter.

This is especially true because few applicants give much thought to their cover letters, even though they have put blood, sweat and tears into their resumes. As the applicant who has taken pains to write a striking letter, you will stand out.

The cover letter is particularly useful if you don't have much relevant experience to put into a resume. It takes a lot less effort to write a cover letter that demonstrates you're the right person for the job despite your lack of experience than it does to actually obtain enough experience to beef up a skimpy resume.

A cover letter highlights the aspects of your experience that are most useful to the potential employer, and you can earn points for knowing what those aspects are. Employers get hundreds of resumes, especially when they advertise a choice position. Employers are also very busy. Often the person screening resumes scans each for only a few seconds. Your cover letter can call attention to the skills, talents, and experience the employer is looking for.

Your cover letter provides the opportunity to show what you know about the field you're interested in and the company you're writing to, as well as your written communication skills. Although some positions put a higher premium on writing skills than others, there are few positions in which the ability to write clearly is not an asset. A well-constructed cover letter can also demonstrate your ability to organize your thoughts and get to the point.

Your letter can explain things that your resume can't. If there are large gaps in your employment history or you are reentering the job market or changing the focus of your career, a cover letter can explain these circumstances in a positive way.

A cover letter can serve the same function as the "job objective" on your resume, and expand upon it. Some applicants are reluctant to limit themselves by putting an objective on their resume. Although it is best for a job-seeker to target the type of work desired as specifically as possible, you may be open to more than one option. Instead of using only one objective on your resume—which you are not likely to tailor to each individual employer—you can vary your objective by the way you express it in your cover letter.

Finally, a cover letter is a little window into your personality. A good cover letter can suggest to an employer, "I'd like to interview this person; they sound like someone I'd like to get to know better. This seems like just the kind of dynamic person this company needs."

A cover letter is perhaps the most important part of a direct-mail sales package. The product is you. As with any other sales letter, you are trying to motivate a specific action. You want that employer to call and invite you for an interview. A dynamic cover letter can arrest his attention and arouse his interest.

Three Kinds of Cover Letters

There are roughly three kinds of cover letters, each corresponding to a different method of job-hunting. Most successful job-seekers will find that they do not employ any one method or use any one kind of cover letter, but rather a combination of all three. To understand the three kinds of cover letters, it is helpful to look at these three types of job search.

Only about one-fifth of the job market is what we call "open." That means that only about 20 percent of job openings are ever publicly

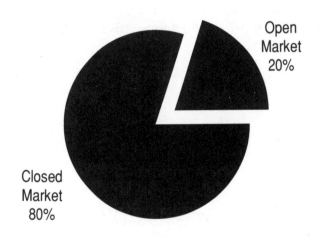

Open Market 20%

Closed Market 80%

known. The main avenue for informing the public about these openings is through want ads in the newspaper, trade magazines, and other publications. Employment agencies and executive-search firms are another source of open-market positions. The first kind of cover letter is the **invited letter,** which is generally a response to a want ad.

The other fourth-fifths of the market is "closed," meaning you can't find out about the positions unless you dig. That digging most often takes the form of compiling a list of all the companies in your field that you might be interested in working for and contacting them to ask

for an interview. Obviously, that means some job-seekers will send out a great many resumes, accompanied by the type of cover letter that we call the **uninvited** or **cold-contact letter,** sometimes blanketing a given field of companies with direct-mail packages.

The successful job-hunter will be persistent in following up on the interviews he or she asks for, even when the employer says there are no openings. Will the employer be annoyed with you for persisting in seeking an interview? Probably not—employers admire drive and ambition. Your persistence means you truly want to work for that company. When I was hiring, the "squeaky wheel gets the grease" approach worked on me almost every time.

A job-hunter who can get a few minutes of an employer's time can succeed in a number of ways. By finding out more about the company's needs, you may be able to create a position for yourself even though the employer has said no openings exist. More likely, however, you will learn a little more about your field, knowledge that you can apply to your job search.

Best of all, you can close the interview by saying, "I'm sorry to hear you have no openings, but perhaps you could suggest someone else in the field who does." If you've made a good impression in your interview, chances are the employer will give you not just one but several referrals.

And that leads us to the third kind of cover letter, a very close cousin to the uninvited letter. This letter, too, is uninvited but it has an edge. It prominently displays the name of a person your addressee knows. We call this kind of cover letter the **referral letter.** Referral letters are the product of "networking," which many experts say is the most effective method of job-hunting.

A referral letter will start out, for example, "John Ross of Technology Unlimited suggested you might have openings for systems analysts."

Referral letters can come about from a number of different sources. You might talk with someone at a meeting of a trade association in your field who will tell you of an opening she knows of. An acquaintance at a party might tell you of someone he knows whose company could use an employee with your experience. A friend might tell you about a job she saw through her company's internal job-posting.

The method of job-hunting you choose will depend a great deal on your situation. If you already have a job and are interested in moving on but not desperate to get a new job, you may be content to read the help-wanted ads in your Sunday newspaper and respond to those that appeal to you.

If, however, you are mounting a major job search or are a recent graduate, you will probably conduct a more aggressive mass-mailing campaign, as well as monitoring the want ads closely and networking to seek contacts who can refer you to where the openings might be.

Next, we'll look at some of the characteristics peculiar to each kind of cover letter.

The Uninvited or Cold Contact Cover Letter

The uninvited letter is the most straightforward and has several advantages. It enables you to learn the exact name of the person who has the power to give you a job. This is a key point. Whenever possible, any cover letter should be sent to a named individual. The largest employer in Central Florida, for instance, throws away any letter that does not address him by name. If you want to get an interview and hence a job, you can forget about using such salutations as "Dear Sir or Madam," "Gentlemen," "Dear Personnel Director," or "To Whom it May Concern." Those salutations tell the employer that you were not concerned enough to find out whom it concerns. We'll talk later about how to find out the name of the best person to address.

The uninvited cover letter provides an opportunity to show what you know about the company you're writing to. Demonstrating that you've done your homework is a good way to get a real edge on your competition. How many times, after all, have you been asked during an interview, "What do you know about our company?" Many employers use your knowledge of the company as a litmus test.

The uninvited cover letter enables you to take a proactive approach to job-hunting instead of the reactive approach, in which you merely answer ads. It can be a great tool for uncovering hidden jobs where supposedly no openings exist. Your letter can make such an impression that you'll be remembered as soon as there is an opening. You may also be able to create an opening for yourself by convincing the employer that they need someone with your talents. At the very least, you may obtain an interview in which the employer can refer you to others in the field who might have use for you.

The biggest disadvantage of the uninvited cover letter is that it is, after all, uninvited. When an employer doesn't have a current opening and hasn't solicited your letter and resume, he is likely to give it much less attention than if there had been an advertised opening. You can minimize this disadvantage by writing a letter that lets the employer know that you are someone he or she should pay attention to.

A key aspect of a successful direct-mail campaign with this letter is compiling a large list of potential employers—perhaps as many as several hundred. You must also research each company, to individualize your letters. We won't deal too extensively here with list compilation and research since our main focus is cover letters. A number of good books, however, offer general job-hunting techniques and deal extensively with developing job leads and researching potential employers. Several of these books are cited in Recommended Reading, page 98. You'll also find a list of sources for job leads on page 33.

The Invited Cover Letter

A cover letter that is invited through a want ad offers the primary advantage that the employer expects and welcomes it; he or she has an opening, may be very anxious to fill it, and is hoping you will be the right person.

The invited cover letter also enables you to speak to the requirements of the ad. You can give the employer what he is looking for because you know what he is looking for; he has spelled it out in his ad.

Whether or not you can write to a specific individual and demonstrate your knowledge of the company the same way you can with the uninvited letter depends on which of two types of want ad you are responding to.

Many want ads reveal the name of the company that placed the ad. When you know what company you're responding to, you can use the same strategies as with the uninvited letter: You can research the company and demonstrate your knowledge in your letter, and also find out the best person to write to—unless the ad specifies the person the company wants you to write to.

Sometimes companies, for various reasons, place *blind ads*, which do not identify the company seeking the employee. Companies place these ads because they don't want their current employees to know they are trying to fill a position, or because they expect a large response and don't want the obligation of responding to every applicant.

Some blind ads are more blind than others. Some use initials for the company name. Some use only an address or post office box. In these cases, it may still be possible to find out which company is advertising. If you can do so, you can demonstrate your knowledge of the company, and the employer will most likely be impressed with your resourcefulness in identifying the company.

In her book *Put Your Degree To Work,* Marcia Fox tells a story about an ad that referred applicants to a "J. M. Smith." Only one of 300 respondents bothered to call the company and ask the full name of "J. M. Smith." Janet M. Smith appreciated the single letter addressed to her and was impressed with the motivation of the job-seeker who had gone to the trouble to learn it. That job-seeker was also one of only three people interviewed for the position. The same applies when the ad asks you to write to "Personnel Director." If you know the name of the company, find out who the personnel director is.

The blindest of blind ads gives only a box number at the newspaper carrying the advertisement. The employer rents a box at the newspaper and uses it as an address to which applicants should respond. There is virtually no way to find out what company is advertising. Thus, you can't address your letter to a named individual, and you can't talk about your knowledge of the company.

To whom should you address your letter when you don't who the advertiser is? As mentioned earlier, avoid "To Whom it May Concern." "Gentlemen" is sexist. "Dear Sir or Madam" is acceptable, if a bit stilted and old-fashioned. I have often used "Dear Friends" as a cordial, non-sexist salutation, although some career experts have said it is too informal. My current favorite for blind box-number ads is "Dear Boxholder."

6

The Referral Letter

The value of the referral letter is in its name-dropping. If you can grab the potential employer's attention by mentioning someone he knows and respects in the first line of the letter, you will have gained a terrific advantage over the competition. Some variations on the referral letter include approaches like these:

"I met with Mary Jones last week, and she mentioned that you might have need for someone with a background in book marketing."

"My adviser, Claude Brachfeld, never misses an opportunity to tell me of your innovations in the superconductivity field."

It would be a rare employer who would fail to interview an applicant with such an edge.

There is also such a thing as a self-referred cover letter, which results when you call the employer before sending a cover letter and resume.

Sometimes employers will put their phone number in an ad even though they are really looking for letters and resumes, wishing to do some preliminary screening by phone. They'll ask only those who sound qualified to send their resumes. So, you call up and the employer asks you to send her your resume. When you write to her, you remind her of the conversation:

"I enjoyed chatting with you this morning about the opening in your art department. As you recall, I told you I have the experience with desktop publishing that you're looking for . . ."

There are other occasions when you may find it useful to call the employer and follow up with a self-referred letter. For instance, you might call at the suggestion of a friend who works at the company and says there are openings you would be right for.

Most Common Methods for Filling Job Vacancies

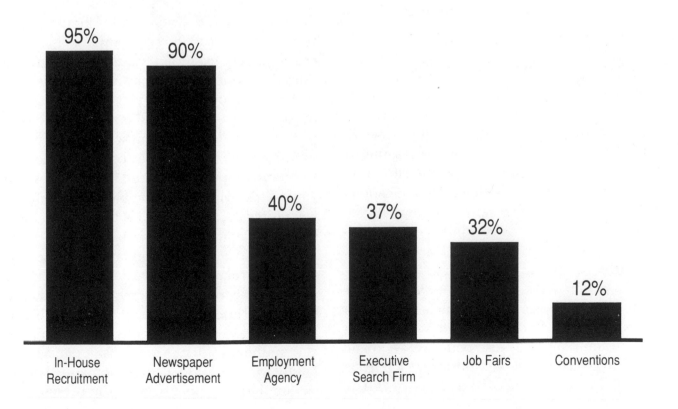

In-House Recruitment	Newspaper Advertisement	Employment Agency	Executive Search Firm	Job Fairs	Conventions
95%	90%	40%	37%	32%	12%

The Basics

There is a formula that can be followed for cover letters. I stress *can* because the most important advice I can give you about this formula and the many sample cover letters at the back of this book is: Don't be afraid to deviate from the formula. Steal phrases, words, and basic structures to your heart's content, but adapt each cover letter to the specific situation. Be a professional and write your own letters.

It's critical that your letter is unique and specific to you—not one that any applicant could have written. Employers can smell a formula a mile away, yet most job-hunters insist on writing letters that sound the same as every other cover letter. As a result, most letters are insufferably dull. You'll make the employer's day if you write an interesting letter. I've had employers call me just to compliment me on my cover letters even when, for one reason or another, they weren't able to hire me.

If you're having trouble getting started, see the worksheets on pages 15 and 17.

The Cover Letter Formula

First paragraph: Tell why you're writing, in such a way as to arouse the employer's interest. Use this paragraph to display your specific knowledge about the company you're writing to.

Second paragraph: Briefly describe your professional and/or academic qualifications. Identify the job title or general area you're interested in. The reader shouldn't have to guess what kind of job you're looking for.

Third paragraph: Relate yourself to the company. Give details as to why you should be considered. Cite examples of your qualifications for the position sought. Draw on the power of your resume and refer to it—but better yet—expand on it. Avoid trite, overused phrases, such as "as you will note in my enclosed resume" or "I have

taken the liberty of enclosing my resume." If you are short on job experience, mention extracurricular activities, especially examples of leadership, special projects you worked on, or the fact that you worked your way through school. If you're a homemaker returning to the workforce, don't forget to include volunteer work and family-management skills.

Fourth paragraph: Request action. Ask for an interview appointment. Suggest a time. Tell the employer that you will call to make an appointment. **[Be sure to follow up!]** It's a lot harder for the employer to ignore a request for action than a wishy-washy "call me if you're interested" approach.

Before closing: Thank the prospective employer for his or her time and consideration.

Dear So and So:
To Whom Should You Send Your Letter?

The best way to find out who should receive your letter is to call the company and ask the receptionist. For example, "Could you tell me who does the hiring for financial analyst positions?" If the receptionist refers you to the personnel department, ask also for the name of the company president. If you must choose between sending your letter to a personnel director and the company president, send it to the president (unless it's a very large company, in which case you should ask for the head of the department in which you're interested in working).

Yes, it's true the president may never see that mail. A secretary or other lower-echelon staffer will probably open and screen the president's mail, but whoever handles it is responsible for responding to the president's mail and making certain the president's image isn't damaged by failing to respond to a correspondent. The underling has to report back to the president on what action was taken; thus a chain of communication is initiated centering around your letter.

Chances are your letter will end up back in the personnel office anyway, but if you send it to the president you will increase the chances of someone with real hiring power seeing it along the way.

Attention-Grabbing Beginnings: The 20-Second Test

The biggest trick to composing a dynamic cover letter is to begin it in a way that will draw the reader in and make him want to read more—and ultimately read your resume and invite you for an interview.

Let's look at it this way: About 500 pieces of paper a week cross the desk of the average busy executive. If he or she spends 25 percent of the work day reading correspondence—and that's a very generous estimate—that means devoting one minute to each piece of paper. But many of those papers represent situations far more urgent to the executive than your cover letter, especially if it's an unsolicited one. You may have as few as 20 seconds to grab his attention.

Some ways to do that include beginning with a quote (see sample page 57), starting with a clever angle (samples, pages 58, 59, and 60), and praising the company you're writing to (sample, page 78).

Quotes

Using a meaningful quote from someone in your field can be an attention-getting way to start your letter. You should be sure that the quote is truly meaningful to the job you're seeking, and was spoken by someone your reader is likely to respect. Also, make sure your quote isn't too long. No matter how good it is, if it's too long your reader is bound to wonder when you're going to get to the point, and maybe put it down halfway through.

Praising the Employer

What employer wouldn't warm up to an applicant who talks about how much he admires the company he's applying to and how much he'd like to work there—and why? Praise for the employer is often a good approach, but you can make it infinitely more credible by supporting your praise with facts that show how much you know about the firm.

The Clever Angle

Once in awhile, you may be able to come up with an approach that is out of the ordinary and shows your creativity (see samples). If you're applying for a job in a creative field. such as journalism, advertising, art, or even sales, you can take more risks than if you're applying as an engineer, for instance. Again, be sure that what you're saying applies to the situation and isn't too long.

Pasting a Copy of the Ad to Your Letter

When responding to a want ad, you can direct your reader's attention to your reason for writing by pasting a copy of the want ad right on the letter. This is particularly effective when writing to a large company that regularly advertises openings, as the recipient can tell immediately which ad you're responding to. Seeing the ad will also refresh his or her memory about what the ad is asking for, and if you've tailored your letter well to the requirements of the ad, your reader just may end up with the impression that you're the perfect person for the job. Obviously, this is not a good approach if your qualifications don't quite match the requirements of the ad.

The Body of the Letter

Your Unique Selling Proposition

There's an advertising term that you should think about when you are composing the body of your letter: the **Unique Selling Proposition,** or USP. When companies are trying to determine how to market a product, they focus on the Unique Selling Proposition, the one thing that makes that product different from any other. It's the one reason they think consumers will buy the product even though it may seem no different from many others just like it. It may be that it has a lower price or more convenient packaging, or it may taste or smell better, or last longer.

When preparing to write a cover letter, you may find it helpful to think about *your* Unique Selling Proposition. What is the one thing that makes you unique? What makes you better from any other candidate applying for a similar position with this company? What can you offer that no other applicant can? What is the one reason the employer should want to hire you above all other candidates? If you can determine your Unique Selling Proposition and build it a dynamic paragraph, you will have a real advantage in creating a dynamic cover letter.

Broadcast Your Accomplishments

To get a great deal of material for the body of your cover letters, make lists of your accomplishments in each of your past positions or in your academic career. Try to list at least three major accomplishments from each position. Think of ways that you left each company or department better than you found it. From that list, choose about three accomplishments that are most relevant to the position you're applying for.

The Screening Process

Remember that when answering ads, you should speak to the requirements of the ad. If your experience does not exactly match what is being asked for in the ad, you can sometimes still make a case for yourself in your cover letter. However, the first person who reads your letter may not have the power and wisdom to decide that you are a worthwhile candidate despite the lack of a perfect match. The first person who reads your letter may be a clerk or other subordinate, screening letters according to whether or not the qualifications match the exact requirements stated in the ad. Therefore, it's important to make the match seem as close as possible. Pick out key phrases and adapt them to your experience.

If the person screening the letter is looking for someone with, say, two to three years of experience, it may actually hurt you if you have considerably more experience because the numbers won't match up. So, you should say you have "more than two to three years experience" so the screener will see the magic "two to three."

Turning a No into a Yes

Imagine an ad that says, "Must have experience placing press releases in publications." Let's say you don't have that particular experience, but all your other qualifications match the requirements of the ad. You *might* decide to write something like this: "Although I don't have experience placing press releases in publications, my experience as an editor has shown me what editors are looking for in the releases they publish." This is a step in the right direction, but a bit too negative.

To develop a more positive, sales-oriented way of addressing the lack of experience in your cover letter, picture an employer asking the same question in an interview: "Do you have experience placing press releases in publications?" If you respond, "No, but my experience as an editor, etc . . ." you automatically have a strike against you because the employer doesn't want to hear "no."

The same thing applies in your cover letter. Don't say: "Although I don't have experience placing press releases in publications . . ." Instead, simply use the rest of the sentence: "My experience as an editor has shown me what editors are looking for in the press releases they publish."

You've turned a "no" into a "yes" and made it look as though you meet the requirements of the ad when you don't quite. Yet, you were completely honest.

The Bottom Line

The job-seeker should always remember that most businesses are there to make money. Employers would like to know that you can help them make money or at least help them not spend so much. Never lose an opportunity to tell the employer how you can make money for him, increase his profitability, boost productivity, achieve greater efficiency, reduce costs, cut waste, or improve sales.

Two Magic Words

There are two words I try not to leave out of any cover letter: "contribution" and "success." I almost always use "contribution" in the first paragraph: "My solid editing experience would enable me to make a meaningful contribution to the managing editor position you are currently advertising." This follows the philosophy of telling the employer what you can do for him, how you can help his bottom line. Employers like the attitude that you want to contribute to his company.

And, nothing succeeds like success. I always make a point of telling the employer how I succeeded in at least one area of my experience. "Success" is a confident word. Employers like an applicant who considers himself a success.

Tips for a Dynamic Format

Employers scan cover letters quickly. Thus, anything you can do to make your special qualifications stand out will give you an edge. Three ways to accent your special qualities are highlighting, quantifying, and demonstrating your ideas.

Highlighting

Some good examples of highlighting can be found on pages 52, 54, 55, and 56 in the sample letters section. These job-seekers have used formats that make their accomplishments stand out—and make it easier for the reader to note them at a glance. Highlighting is also a great technique to use when you are tailoring your letter to the requirements of an ad (the sample letter on page 92 is a nice example of this). One way to do it is by listing special accomplishments and setting them off with bullets, which are those little marks, such as ❑, ●, and ✔. You can also set off your list by indenting it. You can highlight words, phrases and accomplishments by underlining them or making them bold. Most typewriters can't generate bullets, but you can buy them in the form of transfer lettering (also called rub-on lettering) at most art or office-supply stores.

Quantifying

Numbers talk. Sometimes numbers are the best way to drive home a point about your achievements. Tell how many people you supervised, how many customers you handled, how

11

much money you saved the company, by what percentage sales increased in your department during your tenure. You can also say things like:

"I was circulation director for a newspaper with a circulation of 100,000."

"My experience includes creative supervision at the largest ad agency in Tucson."

"I supervised telephone installation requests in the second-largest city in Massachusetts."

Demonstrating your Ideas

An employer can hardly help being impressed by an applicant who has learned so much about the field and/or the company that he can offer his ideas for the company's profitability or efficiency. The best setting for an employer to hear your ideas is in the interview, but to make sure you get the interview, you might want to whet his appetite by revealing a couple of ideas in your cover letter. The example on page 61 shows an excellent example of demonstrating ideas. Remember not to give away too much for free. Just tease the employer with your ingenuity enough so he'll want to hear more.

Closing Your Letter

After thanking the employer for his time and for considering you for a position, you can sign off with any of the standard business-letter closings: "Yours truly," "Very truly yours," or "Sincerely." I use "Cordially" as a friendly approach.

Don't forget to sign your letter. And do sign boldly and confidently—some experts suggest that a black or blue felt-tip pen will produce the proper bold, confident signature.

Do's and Don'ts

DON'T ever send your resume without a cover letter.

DO address your letter to a named individual.

DON'T use a sexist salutation, such as "Gentlemen" when answering a blind ad.

DON'T be negative or too humble.

DO project confidence. For some fields, such as sales or a creative field, it may okay for your confidence to border on cockiness. Just **DON'T** be arrogant.

DON'T use such cliches as "Enclosed please find my resume" or "As you can see on my resume enclosed herewith." Employers can see that your resume is enclosed; they don't need you to tell them. Such trite phrases just waste precious space.

DON'T leave the ball in the employer's court. Don't say things like, "If you are interested in someone with my qualifications, please feel free to call me to arrange an interview" or "I look forward to hearing from you." **DON'T** depend on the employer to take action. Request action.

Request an interview, and tell him when you will follow up to arrange it. Then, **DO SO.** It is imperative that you follow up. You will greatly increase your chances of getting interviews if you call the employer after writing instead of sitting back and waiting for him to call you. Those who wait for the employer to call them will generally have a long wait indeed.

DO make the most of your opening paragraph.

DON'T send a cover letter that contains any typos, misspellings, incorrect grammar or punctuation, smudges, or grease from yesterday's lunch.

DO use simple language and uncomplicated sentence structure. Ruthlessly eliminate all unnecessary words. Follow the journalist's credo: Write tight!

DO speak to the requirements of the job, especially when responding to an ad.

DON'T send letters that are obviously photocopied or otherwise mass-produced. **DO** send an original letter to each employer.

DO imagine yourself in the prospective employer's position. What would you look for in a cover letter? What would turn you off? What would you consider vital information and what would you just as soon see left out?

DO keep it brief. **NEVER, NEVER** more than one page, and it's best to keep it well under a full page. Each paragraph should have no more than four or five sentences. You may think there is important information that you can't possibly leave out, but rest assured, a busy employer will never read it all. The longer your letter appears, the more forbidding it is. If it looks hopelessly long, it may never be read at all.

DON'T write your letter by hand unless the ad requests it.

DON'T tell the employer what he can do for you. **DO** tell him how you can meet his needs and contribute to his company. This is a very common mistake among inexperienced job-hunters. The employer may like to have happy, motivated employees, but he doesn't really care whether you see his company fulfilling your dreams. Generally speaking, he's in business to make a profit; he wants to know how you can help him do that. To paraphrase John F. Kennedy, ask not what the company can do for you, tell what you can do for the company.

If you're a recent grad, **DON'T** forget that the employer's frame of reference is different from a professor's or admissions officer's. He or she may think it's nice that your grade-point average is high or that you got an A in a particularly tough course, but it doesn't really mean a great deal a professional context. They'll be more impressed that you worked your way through school and/or took advantage of every internship opportunity.

DON'T be oversolicitous or plead for favors. Your qualifications should stand on their own.

DO try to answer the question that the employer is going to be asking himself as he reads your letter: "Why should I hire this person?" Answer with your Unique Selling Proposition.

DON'T rehash your resume. You can use your cover letter to highlight the aspects of your resume that are relevant to the position, but you're wasting precious space—and the potential employer's time—if you simply repeat your resume.

DON'T try to include too much detail or be too general. Hone in on the pithy, precise descriptions of the accomplishments that qualify you for the job.

DON'T make the employer dig through the letter to discover what kind of job you're seeking.

DON'T use vague and nebulous phrases that describe your personal objectives: "I am seeking a responsible, people-oriented position with growth potential." Such a description could apply to hundreds of jobs. It's your responsibility to discover which jobs fulfill those requirements.

DON'T expect the employer to offer career counseling. Once in a while, you might run into a benevolent sort who will give you some career advice in an interview. But don't ask for it in a cover letter: "I'd like the opportunity to interview with you so I can clarify my career goals."

DON'T list hobbies or personal interests in your letter unless they are somehow relevant to the position, or you happen to know the person you're writing to is passionate about the same interests. I once knew someone who went through a long series of interviews for a marketing position at a golfing magazine. Just when he was sure he had the job, the magazine rejected him. The reason: He didn't play golf. Nothing he could have said in his cover letter would have gotten him the job, but if he *had* been a golfer and said so in his cover letter, he would have had a clear advantage.

DO be sure the potential employer can reach you. Whenever you know the name of the employer you're writing to, you should follow up and make an interview appointment. However, you should always make sure the employer knows how to reach you in case he wants to call you for an interview before you've had a chance to follow up. If you're writing to a blind-box number, you should, of course, be sure the box-holder knows how to reach you. Your letter should include a phone number that the employer can use to reach you during daytime business hours. It can be your work number if you are able to discretely receive phone calls at your place of employment. It can be your home number if someone is there during the day to answer the phone or if you have an answering machine. Just be sure that whatever number you use is not one that will result in an unanswered phone every time the employer tries to call during business hours.

DO use action verbs. See list below.

Action Verbs

accelerated	distributed	organized	solved
accomplished	doubled	performed	sorted
achieved	eliminated	planned	stabilized
administered	enlarged	prepared	started
analyzed	established	presented	streamlined
approved	examined	processed	strengthened
arranged	expanded	programmed	structured
bought	governed	promoted	succeeded
built	grouped	proposed	summarized
catalogued	guided	purchased	supervised
classified	hired	recommended	systematized
completed	implemented	recruited	trained
conceived	improved	rectified	transacted
conducted	increased	redesigned	translated
consolidated	indexed	reduced costs	trimmed
contracted	interviewed	regulated	tripled
controlled	introduced	reorganized	turned around
coordinated	invented	represented	uncovered
created	investigated	researched	unified
decreased	launched	reshaped	unraveled
delivered	maintained	revised	widened
demonstrated	managed	saved	won
designed	moderated	scheduled	wrote
developed	monitored	serviced	
devised	negotiated	simplified	
directed	orchestrated	sold	

A Cover Letter Worksheet

The hardest part of writing a cover letter is getting started. If you're having trouble, a worksheet like the one below may get you going. The example below shows how one job-seeker filled out the worksheet. The following page shows the letter that resulted from this worksheet. On page 17 is a blank, which you may want to photocopy and use to get started on your own letters.

Remember that the worksheet merely provides the skeleton. Once you have the bare bones, you need to develop the letter.

Cover Letter Worksheet

I am a _recent graduate of Wesleyan College with B.A. in hotel management_

I want a job as _hotel/motel management trainee_

Here's what I can do for your company (my Unique Selling Proposition):

Summer internship with Hyatt Hotels, getting 'real world' experience

Two years working all phases of hospitality at college-run hotel

Developed cost-efficient check-in/check-out system that cuts waste

3.8/4.0 GPA while holding down two jobs to pay for education

Hard-working, conscientious, reliable

Winner of Outstanding Graduate Award, Hilton School of Hotel Management

I will contact you _next week_ to set up an interview.

Thank you for your time and consideration.

The Resulting Letter

435 Shoreline Drive
Charleston, SC 29407
803-555-0303

Mr. Roger G. Harlin
National Hotels
2371 Peachtree Lane, NE
Atlanta, GA 30306

Dear Mr. Harlin,

I'd like to contribute my sharp hotel-management skills, gained through years of experience and my B.A. in hospitality management as a management trainee with your hotel chain.

I'm a recent graduate from Wesleyan College—with a grade-point average of 3.8 out of 4.0—and several years of relevant experience, including:

—Two years in varying levels learning all phases of hospitality management at college-managed hotel.

—Summer internship with Hyatt Hotels.

I have put this experience to good use, first in developing a cost-efficient check-in/check-out system that cut down on waste, saving the college-run hotel an average $5 per guest.

Second, because of this proven innovation and leadership, I won the Outstanding Graduate Award.

I am hard-working, conscientious, and reliable, and I want to put this knowledge and experience to work for your hotel chain.

I will contact you next week to set up an interview.

Thank you for your time and consideration.

Sincerely,

John Donovan

Your Own Worksheet

I am a _____

I want a job as _____

Here's what I can do for your company (my Unique Selling Proposition):

_____

_____

_____

_____

_____

_____

I will contact you _____ to set up an interview.

Thank you for your time and consideration.

Editing

After you've composed your cover letter, you should take a red pencil to it and edit mercilessly. Eliminate every unnecessary word. The more concise you can make your letter, the clearer your message will be: short, sweet, and to the point. The more you can say in the least number of words, the more likely the employer is to read and pay attention to your letter.

On the next two pages are a too-long cover letter and its edited, concise version. The job-seeker who wrote it tried to crowd his letter with too much unnecessary detail.

Mr. Salvador was justifiably proud of his academic career. As he indicates in his last paragraph, *he believes* his background could be useful at a newspaper. But his letter has done nothing to convince the prospective employer that there is any connection between his academic achievements and what he could do for a newspaper. He may well have a vision of how his academic background would relate to being a municipal reporter or sportswriter, but he has done nothing in his letter to relate his college background to the job. Instead, he has told his entire academic history, although little of it has any relevance to the job he is seeking.

His other problem is that his sentences are too long and wordy. The original letter was so long that it went to two pages, a definite no-no in cover letters. Note that, even squeezed onto one page, it is far too wordy and beside-the-point. He needed to remember that his frame of reference, the academic world, is probably very different from the employer's. What sounds impressive in academia may elicit no more than a yawn from any employer seeking an experienced candidate.

A must-have source on concise writing and correct word usage is the classic *Elements of Style* by William Strunk and E. B. White. Macmillan puts out an inexpensive paperback edition. Get it.

After you've cut your letter down to size and proofed it carefully for typos, spelling, grammar, syntax, punctuation, and capitalization, put it down for a few hours (if your time frame allows.) Come back later and read it as though you were the employer. Does it grab you? Is it compelling? Would it make you want to call the applicant in for an interview?

You can also ask a friend to read your cover letter, ideally someone who has experience screening and hiring, or someone in your field.

Well-known ad executive Jane Trahey had a unique method for discovering her letters' impact. She would write her letter, stick it in an envelope, and mail it to herself. By the time it arrived, she would have virtually forgotten sending it and could approach it with the same degree of subjectivity as a prospective employer.

A Letter in Need of Editing

Mrs. Karen Harper
Editor, Wonderful Publications
P.O. Box 185
Secaucus, NJ 07001

Dear Mrs. Harper,

I am interested in applying for the entry-level Municipal Reporting and Sportswriter positions advertised in the September 18, 1986 edition of the Nutville Post. In October of 1985, I graduated from Drew University in Madison, New Jersey, with a Master of Arts Degree in political science. In May of 1984, I graduated from Rutgers University with Bachelor of Arts degrees in political science and history. Since my October graduation, I have furthered my studies by completing several courses at Montclair State College.

Enclosed is my resume, which will give you an idea of my interests and achievements in the public affairs and communications areas. Please note that while attending Drew University, I was selected to participate in the Semester on the United Nations program. Twice weekly, I studied at the United Nations and the Drew facilities on United Nations Plaza in a program that included briefings and addresses by members of the Secretariat, the delegations, the specialized agencies and the nongovernmental organizations represented at the United Nations. Furthermore, please note that while attending Rutgers University, I was selected to join the Iota-Alpha Chapter of Phi Alpha Theta, the International Council of Conspicuous Attainments and Scholarship in the Field of History.

In addition, please note that in selecting my curricula, I emphasized creative writing and development of oral communications skills. As a result, I am able to structure a problem into question form, provide a thesis answer, and support my thesis through qualitative and quantitative methods. Moreover, my three years on the Rutgers University Student Governing Association, two years as president and treasurer of the Rutgers University Political Science Club, and graduate training on team projects at Drew University have given me the ability to address large groups with enthusiasm and clarity.

Similarly, please note that while attending St. Bonaventure High School in Newark, I was selected to serve a three-year term as the boys basketball scorekeeper/statistician and sports-information director. As a consequence, a portion of my responsibilities included the preparation and dissemination of sports information to The Newark Star-Ledger and the Jersey Journal.

Without hesitation, please contact the following three gentlemen for references: Dr. Walter Miller—201-555-3000. Dr. Kenneth Cowell—201-555-5105. Dr. David Wicker—201-555-6485.

Since I believe my background could be utilized very effectively by your newspaper, I hope to hear from you regarding a personal interview.

Cordially,

Peter Salvador

The Edited Version

Mrs. Karen Harper
Editor, Wonderful Publications
P.O. Box 185
Secaucus, NJ 07005

Dear Mrs. Harper,

My strong academic background in political science and government would enable me to make a significant contribution to the municipal reporting position you are currently advertising.

Municipal reporting requires the ability to translate complex governmental issues into simple language for the layman. My academic career has made me well-versed in government issues. My special ability to study and communicate about public affairs was recognized when I was chosen to participate in a special United Nations study program and selected for membership in a history honor society.

My courses also emphasized creative writing and development of oral communications skills, which would enable me to ask politicians the right questions and communicate the issues clearly to readers.

My leadership abilities and skill in working as a team-player may be of eventual interest to you as you are promoting reporters to editing positions. I have been involved in student government, held office in a political-science club and worked on team projects during my graduate training.

I also am interested in the sportswriting position you advertised, and my three years as a school team statistician and sports-information director show I am equally capable of communicating about sports. I demonstrated my ability to assemble sports material for publication by preparing team reports for the Newark Star-Ledger and the Jersey Journal.

I'll give you a call early next week to arrange a personal interview.

Cordially,

Peter Salvador

Pleonasms

A pleonasm is the use of more words than are necessary to express an idea. Eliminate all unnecessary words. Go through your letters and cut out all extraneous words and phrases—then, go through and do it again. See below for a list of common pleonasms and how they can be shortened.

Pleonastic	Tight
in light of the fact	since, because
for recycling purposes	for recycling
one particular youngster	one youngster, a youngster
on a daily basis	daily
a Career Fair to be held May 15	a Career Fair May 15
symposium, which will be held on October 20	symposium October 20
in the lobby itself	in the lobby
during the period of time	when
at this point in time, at the present time	now (even "now" may be unnecessary)
in order to, in an effort to	to
for the purpose of	for
graphics department, which is located in the Knott Building	graphics department in the Knott Building
end result	result
utilized (not so much pleonastic as jargony)	used

Mechanics

So, you've composed the perfect cover letter . . . good for you! Now you need to determine how you'll type it, what kind of paper you'll type it on, what kind of envelope you'll mail it in, and even when you should mail it.

Typing Options

Each cover letter you send must be—or appear to be—a freshly typed original. If you're sending out a lot of cover letters, typing each one individually can be a problem if you are not a great typist. It becomes even more of a problem when you realize each letter must be absolutely flawless. What are your alternatives if you don't type well?

❑ You can hire a typing service or resume company to type them for you. Doing so, however, can be expensive if you are mounting a mass mailing to cold contacts or if your job search takes a while and you are regularly answering many ads.

❑ You can rent a high-quality electric or electronic typewriter or word-processor. Many copy shops and libraries, especially in college towns, have in-house typewriters that you can rent by the hour for use on the premises. Make sure the equipment can make corrections that will be undetectable to your recipients.

❑ You can buy, rent, or borrow a computer whose software handles word-processing functions (or hire someone who has one). Many computer stores will allow you to lease on a fairly short-term basis. Most personal computers are relatively easy to learn, even for someone without a "high-tech" orientation, and chances are the store will offer training. Computerized word processing allows you to type your entire letter and then make all corrections and perfect the layout before you print it out. A computer is your best bet—if you can afford it—especially for mass mailings. You can write virtually the same letter to any number of employers, inserting individual names, addresses, and perhaps interchangeable paragraphs that demonstrate your knowledge of each company.

If You Must Use a Typewriter . . .

Beg, borrow, or buy the best one you can. An electronic typewriter with a film ribbon and a correcting feature is best. If the best you can do is a clunky old manual with a fabric ribbon, at least clean the keys and buy a fresh new ribbon. If you make a mistake, you might be able to get away with one tiny fix with correcting fluid (such as Liquid Paper or Wite-Out) or correction paper (such a Ko-Rec-Type)—but you're better off retyping the letter. There is one trick you can try, however, if you're a lousy typist. Go ahead and make your corrections with correcting fluid, but before signing, have your corrected letter copied onto nice paper at a copy shop using a high-quality machine. The copy will look like an original and the corrections will no longer be visible.

If You Use a Computer (or hire someone to do so) . . .

Consider using the best printer you can afford. You can always put your letter on a disc and have a high-quality printout made at a copy shop or computer store.

The least expensive printer produces **dot-matrix** type. That is type made up, as the name implies, of little dots. There are degrees of quality even among dot-matrix printers. The more dots per inch, the better. Dot-matrix printers are generally acceptable for cover letters, but they are not the best choice.

The next step up is a printer that produces **letter-quality print** (LQP). It, too, produces type made up of dots, but they are configured so they look pretty close to what would come out of a good typewriter, although the image is more gray than black.

The **daisy-wheel** printer produces type identical to what comes out of a good typewriter.

Finally, there is the state-of-the art, the **laser** printer or **laser-jet** printer, which produces a sharp, clear image. A laser printer offer many options in type, graphics, and type of paper.

Paper

For purity and simplicity, nothing beats the classic white 8 1/2 x 11 bond paper, with a 25 percent rag or cotton content. You can't lose by using it. However, many variations are acceptable: ivory, cream, buff, gray, light blue, and tan are all perfectly respectable cover-letter colors. You can also use a textured finish, such as "laid" or "linen." The standard advice is not to use any really flamboyant color, but you could probably get away with an off-beat color if you're applying for a job in a creative field. You don't even really need to use a rag-content bond. The kind of bond paper used in most office copiers should be acceptable in most cases, except for professions such as law. But here's what's not acceptable:

❑ **Paper of a nonstandard size.** Some job-seekers send letters on 8 1/2 by 14 paper (legal size) or 7 x 10 (monarch size) or some other odd size in the hope of making their letter stand out. All you really succeed in doing with a non-standard size is annoying the employer because your letter sticks out of the stack, falls out of the pile, or is hard to file.

❑ **Social stationery.** It should go without saying that scents, flowers, and cartoon-decorated stationery have no place in the business world.

❑ **Your current company letterhead.** I once read an article that actually advised job-seekers to write their cover letters on their current employer's letterhead to prove they were employed. If I were an employer receiving a cover letter on company letterhead, the message would be: "This person steals supplies from his company. He would probably steal them from me, too."

❑ **Corrasable or onionskin paper.** Corrasable paper, which has a slick, shiny surface that is easy to erase, does not make a very professional appearance. And onionskin is too thin and flimsy.

Envelopes

The standard #9 or #10 envelope, either white or a color and texture matching your cover letter/resume stationery, is best. If you have many enclosures, such as writing samples, lists of references and a salary history, a 9 x 12 envelope is acceptable, and keeps the materials within flat. By the time the person with hiring power gets your letter, the envelope will most likely be long gone, so it is a fairly unimportant part of your sales package.

The Perfect Package

If you can afford it, the following makes a terrific package that may impress an employer:

❑ Your cover letter typed on a personalized letterhead

❑ Your resume on a matching letterhead of the same type of paper

❑ An envelope in matching paper with your name and return address printed in the left-hand corner

❑ An attractive commemorative stamp

Although this sort of presentation may give you the ever-so-slightest edge, the advantage compared to the expense is probably negligible. Therefore, I stress that such a package is completely unnecessary. Its real advantage is to make you feel good about the image you're presenting. High morale and self-esteem are crucial in the job search.

When to Mail

Since the best and most plentiful want ads appear in the Sunday newspaper, you are likely to be writing cover letters that day. Should you mail them right away? The answer is an unequivocal yes when you are responding to a blind-box number ad, for the simple reason that the employer has rented the box for only a limited amount of time, sometimes as little as a week. For other ads, you may be better off mailing your letter as late as Tuesday so it won't get lost in the pack of letters that other job seekers mailed Sunday to arrive Tuesday. I always found I could pay more attention to the stragglers that came after the bulk of ad responses. For cold-contact mailings, some career experts have suggested you target your letters to arrive between Tuesday and Thursday, the days the power person is most likely to be at his or her desk. Tuesday has also been cited as an attractive day because it is a lighter mail day in business. The Christmas season, between Thanksgiving and New Year's Day is likely to get the least attention, so avoid this time and any other weeks with holidays in them, if you can.

Delivery Stunts

You can sometimes make an impression by having your letter hand-delivered by messenger (if the employer is in the same city) or air-expressed to another city. Neither method is cheap, but if it's the job of your dreams and there is a special reason for you to respond quickly, you may want to spring for one of these methods. If your primary motive is to impress the employer with the trouble and expense you've gone to, be aware that it may be the secretary and not the power person who knows you used a special kind of delivery.

Some career experts have suggested you can gain an advantage by marking "Personal" or "Confidential" on the envelope and even go so far as leaving your return address off. The idea is to keep a secretary from screening your letter and to arouse the employer's curiosity. Use this technique, however, at your own risk since many employers may be more annoyed than intrigued.

Keeping a Record

It's a very good idea to keep a record of every cover letter you send out so you know when you need to follow up with which employers. There are three easy ways to keep a record.

1. Make a photocopy of every letter you send. If you have been pasting a copy of the want ad to your letter, you'll also have a record of the ad. Another good reason to make copies of your letters is that if you're not producing them on a machine with a memory (such as an electronic typewriter or computer), keeping copies will allow you to recycle paragraphs in future letters.

2. Since it's not always convenient—or cheap—to make a copy of every letter, consider buying a pad of columnar-ruled paper (or just making some vertical rule lines on notebook paper). You can make a column each for: position, company name and address (if known), name of contact person and phone number for follow-up, date you sent your cover letter/resume and what follow-up action you took. You can also record the history of each cover letter/resume on an index card.

3. You can photocopy the chart on page 25.

Job Search Log

Company Name / Position	Contact	Phone	Date	Result	Follow-up

Using Cover Letters Creatively

You can expand your networking opportunities by writing cover letters to organizations other than direct employers and making other creative uses of your cover letters.

❑ **Letters to your college placement service.** Such letters are particularly practical after you've graduated and moved away from your college town. A well-written letter will impress your placement officer and possibly get you preferential treatment. Some placement offices also serve non-alumni. See sample, page 48.

❑ **Letters to professional and trade organizations.** Almost all professional and trade organizations have some type of placement service, whether they make your resume available to member companies, publish situation-wanted ads in the group's newsletter or run a job hotline. Sometimes there is a charge for the service, sometimes not. You can send your resume with a nice cover letter to all the organizations in your field. Don't forget general professional organizations for women and minorities, such as Business and Professional Women's Association or the National Association of Black Law Enforcement Officers. Sample, page 49.

❑ **Letters to employment agencies.** Employment agencies frequently advertise just as direct employers do, and it should be noted that 10 percent of job-hunters at the managerial and executive level get jobs through employment agencies and executive-search firms. You can answer their ads with a cover letter that is not substantially different from one you would send an employer. The only difference is you should acknowledge that you are applying for a position with the agency's client company. You can also write cold-contact letters to agencies, especially those specializing in your field. This is not a particularly effective way to find a job, but in an extensive job search, it is another way to ensure you have covered all the bases. You will have considerably better luck if you follow up these uninvited letters to agencies with phone calls. Sample, page 50.

❑ **Letters to executive-search firms.** Job-seekers generally don't seek out search firms: instead, executive-search firms rely on contacts in the business world to refer candidates who will fill the needs of their client companies. These companies usually keep search firms on retainer. However, it never hurts to send your resume to an executive-search firm, especially if you are able to use the referral-letter approach. Sample, page 51.

❑ **Sending a letter without a resume.** Some experts suggest you send a letter without a resume because when many employers see a resume with a letter, they assume you are unemployed and sending similar mailings to a number of people. If you can summarize relevant highlights of your experience in a letter so well-written that the employer will want to talk with you further, you may be better off not sending a resume. That way your correspondence will seem more like a business letter than the run-of-the-mill resume mailing, just like the hundreds of others that cross the employer's desk. You can ask for a meeting instead of an interview.

❑ **Responding to a hidden opportunity in an ad.** You might see an ad for a position you're not qualified for, but you can see a hidden opportunity in the ad. For instance, one woman saw an ad for a museum-director position that she did not qualify for, but since it was in the natural-history field, where she did have considerable experience, she wrote a letter suggesting she would make a great assistant to the new director. She got the job. The same thing worked for me when I saw an ad seeking people to sell advertising space for a new magazine. I wasn't interested in selling, but I knew that after some ads were sold, the magazine would need an editorial staff. I wrote offering my editorial services, and I, too, was successful in creating a position for myself.

Sticky Issues

What if an ad asks for salary requirements or history?

The request for salary requirements is a common problem in the writing of cover letters, especially responses to blind-box number ads. Employers often use blind-box ads as a way to screen out applicants who want a bigger salary than the company feels it can or wants to pay. The employer asks you to put your salary requirement in your cover letter, and if you want too much money, he probably won't call you for an interview. You don't know who he is, so there's no reason for him to bother sending you a polite rejection letter.

If salary is the most important issue to you, you have no problem. You can put your salary requirement in your cover letter with no qualms because if the employer eliminates you, you will have lost nothing because you don't want to work for less than your required salary anyway.

If, however, the job itself is important to you and you are flexible about salary, you have more of a problem. The perfect job could be advertised. You really want it, but the blind-box ad asks for a salary requirement. If you put down your ideal salary, you risk being eliminated from a job you'd love to have.

Your choices:

❏ You could skirt the issue entirely by either leaving out the salary requirement or saying:

"My salary requirement is negotiable."

Or: "I am earning the market value for a systems analyst with four years of experience. I would be happy to discuss my compensation requirement in an interview."

Be aware, however, that some advertisers put the disclaimer in their ads that no applicant will be considered without a salary requirement.

❏ You could state your current salary and say it is negotiable.

"I am currently earning an annual salary of $25,000, and my salary requirement is negotiable."

That way, if the company is planning to pay less than your current salary, chances are you don't want the job no matter how wonderful it is.

❏ You could give a range, for which the low-end figure is 10 percent above your current or last salary.

An employer who asks for a salary history, is trying to determine the size and frequency of raises you are accustomed to. It is usually safe to either send a salary history (do it on a separate sheet so you don't take up space in your cover letter) or simply tell your current salary.

Should you include references in your cover letter?

No. References belong in the interview phase of job-hunting, so they should not be listed in your resume or cover letter. Occasionally, an ad will specify that you must send references. In that case, it is probably best to list them on a separate sheet rather than take up precious space in your cover letter. You can, of course, refer to the sheet in your letter. ("A list of references is enclosed.")

Should you send letters of recommendation?

Generally no. Letters of recommendation have little credibility because anyone who would write you a letter of recommendation wouldn't say anything negative about you.

Should you explain negative aspects of your job history?

Another tough question. In the beginning of this book, I said the cover letter is an opportunity to explain the negatives. However, I must caution you to bring up any negatives extremely judiciously. Most are better handled in the interview, and you can wait for the employer to bring them up instead of calling attention to something they might not have noticed.

Chances are, whatever "problem" you think there might be with your job history is probably in your head, or at least a lot more important to you than to the prospective employer. There is no point to making your problem into his problem. When in doubt, leave it out.

Don't say anything about not having enough experience. Make the most of the experience you do have and let employers judge for themselves.

Don't mention any negative circumstances of leaving any of your past jobs. The sample letter on page 70 gets off to a horrendous start by telling the employer *in the first sentence* that the applicant was laid off from his last job. What a turnoff.

It is probably not necessary to point out lack of educational qualifications. The sample letter on page 75 goes into an elaborate, if well-expressed, plea for the employer to consider her even though she does not have the degree mentioned in the ad as a requirement. I believe the writer would have been better off omitting that paragraph. She could have let her otherwise good cover letter and fine resume stand on their own merits. If the employer was impressed with her experience, he might not have even looked at her educational background. If he liked her letter and resume, he might have decided that a degree really wasn't important for doing the job.

It can't hurt to briefly explain why you are making a career switch, especially if you are making a radical shift from one field to another. Samples on pages 88 and 90 show effective ways to explain career shifts.

Thank-You Letters

Terrific. You got an interview. Now, the minute you get home, do not pass Go, do not collect $200. Instead, sit down and write a thank-you letter to the employer while the interview is fresh in your mind. If you know the employer is planning a quick decision, you may want to make special arrangements to have your thank-you letter delivered quickly, such as hiring a messenger service or even hand-delivering the letter to the employer's secretary.

Thanking a prospective employer for his or her time is just common courtesy. But, a thank-you letter can do more:

❏ It's a way to keep your name in front of the employer.

❏ It's a way to build on the strengths of the interview and emphasize the match between you and the job, especially now that you know more about the company.

❏ It's a way to bring up anything you thought of after the interview that is pertinent to the employer's concerns.

❏ If you are extremely careful, you may be able to address anything that went badly in the interview and try to correct it.

❏ If the employer has asked for additional materials that you didn't bring to the interview (references, writing samples, etc.) you can send a thank-you letter with the items.

❏ It's a way to restate your understanding of the next step in the process. ("I look forward to meeting with your vice president, Mrs. Green, sometime next week.")

❏ It's an opportunity to restate your interest in and enthusiasm for the job.

❏ It's another chance to show how well you express yourself.

But the best thing about thank-you letters is that, even though virtually every book on job-hunting advises sending thank-you letters, very few job-seekers actually do so. If you're one of the few that do, you're bound to have an edge.

See sample thank-you letters beginning on page 94.

When you get a rejection letter without an interview or after an interview

Write back to thank the employer for acknowledging your letter or thank him again for the interview. Encourage the company to make good on its promise to keep your resume on file. The employer will be impressed with your courtesy and continuing interest. You'll keep the dialogue going with the company, and your name will more likely be remembered the next time there's an opening.

Sample follow-up to a rejection letter

```
                                        34 Easy Street
                                        St. Joseph, MO 64503
                                        816-555-4334

Ms. Suzanne Lee
Rehabilitation Hospital
10 Medical Court
St. Louis, MO 63188

Dear Ms. Lee,

Thank you for your letter dated April 17th. I am disappointed
that because of the reorganization of the department that the
medical records clerk position is no longer available.

I appreciate your offer to keep my resume on file. I am very
interested in working for a leader in medical care such as
Rehabilitation Hospital.

Once again, thank you for your time and consideration. Good luck
in the reorganization, and I hope to hear from you in the near
future.

Sincerely yours,


Deborah S. Stiles
```

Declining Letters

You got a job offer! But, alas, the job is not right for you. The money isn't right, or another offer is better. Write a nice letter turning down the job. You never know when you might need that employer again, so you want to stay in his or her good graces.

Sample Declining Letter

409 Third Avenue
New York, NY 10010
212-555-2121

Mr. Jerry Kudos
American Graphics
12 West 15th Street
New York, NY 10005

Dear Mr. Kudos,

Thank you for all the time you and Ms. Atwood spent considering me for a position as a graphic artist. I sincerely appreciate your consideration—as well as that of your staff members who spent time with me during this process.

I most appreciate your offer of employment, however, after much deliberation and careful analysis, I must respectfully decline your offer. I feel another opportunity better matches my qualifications and career path.

This has been a very difficult decision; yours was an outstanding opportunity.

I hope our paths will cross again in the future. You have been most kind, and I again thank you for your time and consideration.

Sincerely,

Mary Beth Rider

Acceptance Letters

It's the moment we've all been waiting for! You got an offer, and it's the perfect job! You've decided to go for it. Congratulations! It's important to write a letter thanking the employer for the offer and accepting the offer. The most important reason to write an acceptance letter is to state your understanding of the terms of employment: salary, benefits, starting date, perquisites, duties, and so forth. That way, if there is a discrepancy between your understanding and your new employer's, it can be brought out in the open before you start work. It's also a written document that can help if legal difficulties ever arise.

Sample Acceptance Letter

```
                                        145 Kelly Lane
                                        Rochester, NY 14620
                                        716-555-14604


Mr. Jack G. Wallace
Eastman Kodak
Colorfast Drive
Rochester, NY 14604

Dear Mr. Wallace,

Thank you for your telephone call of September 4 offering me a
job as a chemical engineer with your processing department at an
annual salary of $35,000. Please consider this letter my formal
acceptance.

As I mentioned to you, because I am a group leader in a major
experiment with my present company, I will not be able to start
until the middle of October.

The offer fulfills one of my career goals—working for Kodak.

I want to thank you for all your help and consideration. I also
appreciate the help of Dr. Adams and Ms. Graf.

Please let me know if there is any additional information needed
or details I should be aware of prior to my arrival in October.

Cordially,


Darlene P. Hopps
```

Sources of Job Leads

Your newspaper, business magazine, or trade journal contains more than just want ads to help in your job-search. (Don't forget that a company's annual report is often the best source for these same kinds of leads.) Here are other stories to look at when developing a list of contacts for your search.

❏ Stories about products or services in great demand. Companies with hot products may be looking to expand their workforce. You may be able to get in on the ground floor by writing a dynamic cover letter to the company before they advertise for more workers.

❏ Your knowledge of technological breakthroughs, new patents, discoveries, and other developments in an industry or occupation can make a big impression in your letter, especially if you can catch onto the trend before anyone else does.

❏ Most business sections in both business/trade magazines and newspapers run a column listing promotions, retirements, and sometimes terminations and resignations. The out-going person may create an opening you could fill.

❏ Contract awards. When a company successfully bids on the right to manufacture goods or perform services for another company or the government, chances are the company awarded the contract will need more workers.

❏ Major events, such as a world's fair or Olympics in the city in which a company is located (or a company supplying such an event) create job openings.

❏ The opening of a new plant or facility can create opportunities.

❏ Reports of increased sales and earnings, which can be found not only in external publications, but also in the company's own annual report, may signal an expansion of the workforce.

❏ Is the corporate headquarters moving to your city or state? Undoubtedly the firm will need local people to fill openings.

❏ Mergers and acquisitions can create opportunities because many workers leave a merged company in the face of an uncertain future.

❏ Stock underwritings of new and developing companies may foretell opportunities because there will now be capital available to fill openings and create new positions.

❏ Articles on meeting speakers and award-winners can provide fodder for dynamic cover letters.

Source: Jack Erdlen, chairman of Costello, Erdlen & Company; Wellesley, Massachusetts

Checklist

Your cover letter is ready for mailing! Or is it? Compare it to this checklist to see if you've written the most dynamic letter possible.

❑ Is it an original letter rather than a mass-produced copy?

❑ Is it addressed to a named individual? (unless it is a response to a blind ad)

❑ If it's a response to a blind ad, is the salutation nonsexist?

❑ Does the letter grab the reader's attention in the first paragraph?

❑ Is it confident without being arrogant?

❑ Have you left out everything negative?

❑ Is the letter neat and attractive?

❑ Is every word spelled correctly? Is all grammar, syntax, punctuation, and capitalization correct? Is the letter free of typographical errors?

❑ Is it no longer than one page?

❑ Is the letter concise and to the point?

❑ Does it avoid such cliches as "I have taken the liberty of sending my resume enclosed herewith"?

❑ If it's in response to an ad, does the letter speak to the requirements of the position?

❑ Is it interesting?

❑ Does it project the image of a person you would like to get to know better if you were the employer? Have you read it from the employer's perspective?

❑ Have you told the employer what you can do for him rather than what he can do for you?

❑ Have you presented your Unique Selling Proposition?

❑ If you're a recent grad, have you avoided overreliance on an academic frame of reference?

❑ Have you avoided pleading for favors?

❑ Have you avoided getting too detailed?

❑ Have you spelled out what kind of job you're looking for?

❑ Have you avoided rewriting your resume in your cover letter?

❑ Have you avoided describing your personal objectives in vague terms?

❑ Have you avoided asking for career counseling?

❑ Have you avoided listing hobbies or interests unless relevant to the position?

❑ Have you listed accomplishments?

❑ Is it clear where the employer can reach you during business hours? Have you ensured that either a person or a machine will take the employer's call?

❑ Have you used action verbs?

❑ Have you requested action, and told the employer you'll call for an appointment?

❑ Have you signed your name boldly and confidently?

Cover Letter Samples

A Word About these Samples:
There were a couple of ways we could have gone about assembling sample cover letters. We *could* have written fifty samples of perfect cover letters, but we decided you could learn more from real letters. By seeing letters that were written by real applicants, you can see what they do wrong and what they do right. All identities have been changed to protect the privacy of the writers. You can tell which letters are good and which are not so good by the letter grades we've given them. You may notice that there are far more examples of cold-contact letters, and responses to want ads than the other sorts of letter discussed. That's because you will probably have fewer opportunities to use the other types. Please do note that any of the good examples of cold-contact and ad-response letters can be turned into a referral letter simply, by adapting the introductory paragraph to mention to person who referred you. You can get a lot of good ideas for your cover letters from these samples.

The Worst Cover Letter We Ever Received

○ It arrived on shiny corrasable paper, typed in faded gray ink, complete with sexist salutation, misspellings, typos, sentence fragments and nothing that a good cover letter should contain.

○ Grade: F

65 Student Drive
Harrisburg, PA 17103
717-555-2323

Radio WHRS
34532 Highway 22
Harrisburg, PA 17103

Gentlemen:

I am a recent graduate of Harrisburg College; In which I recieved a Bachelor of Arts Degree in Communications. And I would very much like to persue a caree in media.

I have enclosed a copy of my resume' for your review. I would appreciate it very much if you would look it over to see if I meet your standards for employment with your radio station.

I would also appreciate hearing on your decision on employemnt with you. One thing I can promise is that I will Give 100% to my job. Since WHRS is my hometown radio station, I only want to hear thes in it.

Thank you.

Very Truly Yours,

Gilbert David King

Recent Graduate Letter

- Contains too much of what the company can do for him and not enough of what he can do for the company
- Leaves ball in employer's court
- Grade: C-

234 Adobe Pkwy.
Albuquerque, NM 87114
505-555-0000

Mr. Amos Jacoby
Shearson Financial Corp.
5 Main Street
Albuquerque, NM 87114

Dear Mr. Jacoby,

This August I will be graduating from the University of New Mexico with a Bachelor's degree in finance and am seeking an opportunity to use my background. I am writing to ask if you anticipate any such openings at your company in the near future.

Based on my experience working part-time with a local brokerage house, I feel I would be an asset to your company. Becoming a member of your finance staff would fulfill my goal of becoming a professional and would give me the opportunity to grow as a business leader.

Enclosed is a copy of my resume, which shows my qualifications and achievements as a student in the discipline of business and finance.

I am eager to set up an appointment for an interview at your convenience. You may contact me at (505) 555-0000.

Thank you for your consideration.

Sincerely,

Stephen S. Dempsey

Recent Grad Letter

○ Does not address recipient by name
○ Although he takes a novel approach in suggesting an initial interview by phone, he still should take the initiative and say he will call the employer to set up an interview, whether by phone or in person
○ Grade: C-

109 Church Street
Austin, TX 78712
512-555-1212

Personnel Department
Apex Computers, Inc.
50 College Blvd.
Austin, TX 78712

Dear employer/recruiter,

I am a recent college graduate who is looking to enter the computer field. In view of my academic record (3.89/4.0), my program emphasis on computer languages, and my specific interests in computers, I strongly believe that you should consider employing me in the computer pool at Apex Computers, Inc.

Of particular interest to me is the opportunity to offer my related experience in technical and research writing. For example, my senior-year research thesis examined how personal computers could be used in the classroom. My thesis was printed and distributed to all the professors at the university.

My resume is attached. Please feel free to call me to conduct an initial interview by phone. I believe you will be pleased with the skills I can offer Apex Computers. I hope I will soon have the pleasure of talking to you.

Sincerely,

Larry Gangston

Recent Grad Letter

- ○ Shows she knows about the field by expressing her understanding of entry-level positions in the field.
- ○ Uses cliches and jargon
- ○ Throws away impact of decent letter by saying, "If my background seems to fit. . ."
- ○ Grade: C+

2343 Kansas Circle
Fulton, MO 65251
314-555-1314

Mr. Craig Kopaz
Kopaz Communications, Inc.
St. Louis, MO 63188

Dear Mr. Kopaz,

My excellent telephone, organizational, writing and editing skills would enable me to make a key contribution to your firm as a public relations assistant.

As you can see on my resume, I have just graduated from Ohio State University with a major in communications. Though my long-range goals are in the area of writing, I am realistic about the nature of entry-level positions in this field. I have had recent experience in both editing and writing and feel that my background may be of interest to you.

My interest in this area developed while working as a Communications Assistant for the American Red Cross where I was involved in the writing, editing, and layout of chapter newsletters. My interest further developed when researching and writing an employee training manual for Midwest Savings & Loan.

I am most eager to face a challenging position in which to market my employer's services while utilizing my writing and editing skills. The enclosed resume gives some indication of the depth of my academic background and my active working experience. I am confident my record in these areas could be useful to your organization.

If my background seems to fit your needs, please contact me at your convenience.

Your consideration is greatly appreciated.

Cordially,

Sandra Stern

Recent Grad Letter

○ Talks directly about what he can offer the company
○ Plays up the relationship between relevant work experience and putting himself though school
○ References should not be included
○ Letter weakened by leaving ball in employer's court
○ Grade: B-

110 Lambreth Lane
Syracuse, NY 13210
304-555-5555

Dear Mr. MacDonald,

With the completion of my B.A. in Building Construction at Syracuse University and two years experience as a foreman in building, I believe I could be a good estimator with a minimum of training.

A B+ average in all my courses while working twenty hours a week to support myself demonstrates that I would be able to learn your procedures quickly while meeting other work requirements as well. Courses in business and communication would enable me, in time, to also function in a supervisory role for you.

Two years as a successful foreman for Syracuse Home Builders prove I can get along with construction workers, sub-contractors and suppliers, even under construction deadline pressure. Frequent, direct dealing with suppliers and negotiating prices with them would enable me to make realistic estimates.

Dr. Huddard, Mr. Lott and others listed on the enclosed resume would be glad to verify that I can work with enthusiasm and dedication.

I would be grateful if you would tell me a convenient time and place when I may talk with you further about my qualifications as the hard-working estimator you want.

Sincerely,

Jake Johnson

110 First Avenue
Scotsdale, AZ 85251
602-555-3323

Mr. Robert Hogan
Ace Engineering
234A Office Complex
Scotsdale, AZ 85251

Dear Mr. Hogan,

As a recent college graduate, I understandably have not yet had much of an opportunity to gain solid work experience in my field.

Still, as you can see on the enclosed resume, I have gained practical experience in engineering through part-time positions I held while in college and summer internships.

I've known that engineering was to be my career from before I entered college, with the intent to join a prestigious engineering firm such as yours upon graduation.

I believe that my educational and technical background as well as my experience (although it is limited) can be utilized by your firm as an advantage, and look forward to an interview when I may have the opportunity to discuss with you employment possibilities.

May I phone you in the next week for an appointment? I look forward to talking with you soon.

Sincerely,

Robert Krane

Recent Grad Letter

- ○ Should have found out editor's name
- ○ Request for interview is not proactive, although it is a good idea to ask for interview despite lack of openings
- ○ Negative information unnecessary
- ○ Resulted in an interview and job offer
- ○ Grade: B+

4115 H Street, #20
Davis, CA 95616
818-555-4115

Dear Editor,

I am a graduating senior seeking a career in journalism. As managing editor of my award-winning daily collegiate paper, The California Surfer, of the University of California, Pikes Point, I was responsible for overseeing daily operations of the newsroom, including seven desk editors and one night editor. My duties included deciding placement of all stories in the paper, doing daily editing, serving on the editorial board, mitigating personnel problems and serving as liaison with the production and business departments. I also managed our United Press and UC Capitol Bureau wire services.

In addition to my management duties, I wrote approximately four to nine news stories per week, covering a variety of topics including local and student governments. I have also covered state politics and have much experience covering local government at the city and county level. I have also gained great insight into politics at the county level through my current internship with the Orange County Supervisors Office.

The California Surfer, despite being a student newspaper, has the largest daily circulation in Orange County and serves also as a community newspaper, focusing as much attention on local politics as what happens on campus. They also have a full-time reporter covering the events at the state capitol. Thus, I feel that while I have no immediate full-time experience with a professional newspaper, that my excellent, conscientious and thorough writing and reporting skills more than qualify me for a position on your newspaper.

I will be graduating in June and would appreciate being kept in mind if you have any job openings. In addition, I will be in New Jersey on March 27 and 28 and would appreciate being able to stop by and talk with you even if you have no immediate openings. Thank you for your full consideration.

Sincerely,

Allison Cassidy

7 Apple Court
Eugene, OR 97401
503-555-0303

Mr. Archie Weatherby
California Investments Unlimited, Inc.
25 Sacramento Street
San Francisco, CA 94102

Dear Mr. Weatherby,

Please consider this letter as an initial application for
a position as an insurance broker for California
Investments Unlimited, Inc.

I recently graduated from the University of Oregon with a
degree in business, where I was president of the Future
Business Leaders of America.

Although a recent graduate, I am not a typical new
graduate. I attended school in Michigan, Arizona and
Oregon. And I've put myself through these schools by
working at such jobs as radio advertising sales and
bartending, both of which enhanced my formal education. I
have the maturity and ability to embark on a career in
insurance brokering, and I'd like to do this in
California, the state I grew up in.

I will be in California at the end of this month and I'd
like very much to talk with you. I will follow up this
letter with a phone call to see if I can arrange a time to
meet with you.

Thank you for your consideration.

Sincerely,

John Oakley

Letter Seeking a Summer Job During College

- ○ Should have learned name to write to
- ○ Nice personalization by talking about her connection with the paper
- ○ Her sincerity about wanting experience more than money will win points with employer
- ○ Grade: A-

317 Tenney Court
West Orange, NJ 07052
201-555-2929

Editor
The Journal
23 Chancelor Street
West Orange, NJ 07052

Dear Sir or Madam,

After spending much time throughout junior high school, high school, and college doing newspaper work, I would like to continue pursuing my interest in journalism with a summer job in the field. I am writing to ask if The Journal has any positions available to college students during the summer months.

This year, as a freshman at Amherst College in Massachusetts, I became a news writer for our student newspaper, The Amherst Student, which is published twice a week. At the start of the second semester, I was promoted to News Editor, a position that gives me the responsibility for the news section for one issue a week. We do all of our own production, so in addition to gathering story ideas, assigning stories, and editing them, I have become skilled at layout techniques.

During my senior year at West Orange High School, I was Editor in Chief of our student paper, The Pioneer. In addition, throughout junior high and high school, I wrote several articles which were published in The Journal. I am mentioned in Brian Orse's article on the high school writing program. Mr. Jenkins pointed to me as a recent WOHS graduate who is following up on journalism training.

I would like to emphasize that I am looking for experience in the "real world" of journalism this summer—salary is not my primary concern. I would greatly appreciate any position that you could offer. I will be home for Spring Break from March 22 - 29 and I would be available for an interview that week. I look forward to hearing from you.

Sincerely,

Linda Shue

Referral Letter

- ○ Somewhat lacking in confidence
- ○ Should have learned more about the opening so she could have better targeted her letter instead of offering a smorgasbord of experience; this makes it too long
- ○ Leaves ball in employer's court
- ○ Grade: B

110 First Street
Alexandria, VA 22306
802-555-5555

Dear Mr. Fouche,

Nancy Jones of Green & Associates Advertising, suggested I contact you regarding the possible public relations opening in your organization.

As an editor/writer for Alexandria's city magazine, I've developed my talent and experience as a public relations writer. I've recently had a lot of encouragement from the local advertising community that I do indeed have talent in that direction.

Because the staff of the magazine was very small, I wore a number of hats. I developed the editorial format and individual story concepts, wrote numerous articles, edited all copy, laid out the magazine and supervised all in-house production.

Another important aspect of my work there was the area of public relations. I prepared numerous press releases and spoke on behalf of the magazine at public gatherings and on radio and TV. I wrote several direct mail pieces, as well as public relations oriented material both for publication in the magazine and about the magazine for publication in other media. I have previously developed a company newsletter for a South Jersey hotel and worked on the departmental training manual at North Jersey Publishing.

My high degree of motivation has been recognized by my previous employers who have quickly promoted me to positions of greater responsibility. I was promoted from assistant editor to editor of Alexandria Monthly after only five months. At North Jersey Publishing, I was rapidly given responsibility for the only two consumer magazines, one of which was the only newsstand magazine, to come out of the company's Newark office.

I would be eager to talk with you about the contribution I could make to your organization. I can make myself available for an interview at your convenience.

Sincerely,

Jane Smithe

Self-Referral—Follow-up to Phone Conversation

○ Good summary of key selling points; summation of phone conversation
○ Quantifies
○ Leaves ball in employer's court, although she makes it clear she expects an interview
○ Grade: B+

4545 Coal Miners Pkwy.
Wheeling, WV 26003
304-555-3030

Mr. Arron Hammersted
Skalers Department Store
300 Main Street
Wheeling, WV 26003

Dear Mr. Hammersted,

Thanks for talking to me on Friday about personnel needs for your store. It's encouraging to know you are about to have three openings.

I'm enclosing my resume with the thought that the next step will be an interview.

I've spent the last three years cultivating my skills and abilities in retail. These years provide a good background for my ultimate goal of a job like yours: running a floor in a department store like Skalers.

My proudest achievement in retail was last year when my department exceeded budgeted sales by more than 200%, thanks to innovative pricing and selling.

My creative thinking and attention to detail are certainly the two qualities that have taken me to where I am today.

I have gotten good reviews from my superiors at the store, but I feel I can do even better at a store such as Skalers—increasing sales and promoting in-store traffic.

I can make myself available for an interview at your convenience. You may reach me during business hours at 304-555-2625.

Thanks, Mr. Hammersted, for considering me for these positions (I'm most interested in the floor manager spot but don't want to rule out department manager). I look forward to hearing from you soon.

Cordially,

Susie Ray Evans

○ Good format for sending inquiry to college placement office and keeping office informed of any changes in current status
○ Grade: A

43 Longhorn Drive
Dallas, TX 75223
214-555-2937

Ms. Alice Dulittle
Placement Office
University of Texas
Austin, TX 78712

Dear Ms. Dulittle,

I am a recent graduate of the University of Texas and am in the job market for a position in nursing. My speciality is in pediatric nursing.

I am hoping that you will keep my file current and inform me when any nursing recruiters are for on-campus interviews or when you hear of openings in my field.

Enclosed is an updated version of my resume for your files. Also please note my new address and telephone number for your records.

Thank you for your help.

Sincerely,

April Brightly

209F N.W. 111th Street
Gainesville, FL 32609
904-555-5665

Mr. Dusty Rhodes
National Magazine Association
3434 Broadway
New York, NY 10022

Dear Mr. Rhodes,

I will be receiving my master's degree in magazine marketing in December and am wondering if your organization might be of help to me regarding placement in the magazine marketing/marketing research field.

My research and thesis have particularly dealt with improving readership studies so they can better define magazine audiences to potential advertisers, which should be of interest to your members.

I am wondering, first, if your organization has a placement service. I am enclosing a resume, but please let me know if there are other forms and if there is a user fee.

Secondly, I am wondering if demand by your members has caused you to compile a list of market research firms available to them, and if so, how I might obtain such a list. Perhaps if you do not have such a list, you might be able to direct me to one.

I greatly appreciate your time and trouble in aiding me with my job search.

Sincerely,

Scott Hent

Employment Agency Letter

- Good use of highlighting
- Good use of quantifying
- Should have taken proactive approach to interview
- Should have obtained name of person to write to
- Grade: B+

15 Irvington Avenue
Irvington-on-Hudson, NY
10533
914-555-1515

Honest Personnel
55 W. 55th Street
New York, NY 10021

Dear Friends,

I have a broad diverse background in telecommunications that could perhaps meet the needs of one or more of your client companies.

I have a unique perspective to offer companies with internal telecommunications departments:

- I have been manager of the telecommunications department of one of the largest computer companies in the country.

- I worked for several years at Bell Labs on the cutting edge of telecommunications equipment.

- I have excellent management and budget experience, and have acted as a liaison between vendors and users in my past two positions.

- In my current position at Hanco Industries, which has annual sales in excess of $5 billion, I oversee a $140 million telecommunications budget.

With this expertise, I am confident I could step into a top management position at one of your client companies.

I am particularly interested in staying in New York, but would consider other areas in the Northeast if the compensation is attractive.

I can make myself available for an interview at your convenience. You may reach me during business hours at 914-555-9675.

Thank you for your consideration.

Sincerely,

Mary Greenwood

34 Forest Drive
Westfield, NJ 07090
201-555-9977

Mr. Ian Stevenson
ExecuSearch
300 Madison Avenue
New York, NY 10036

Dear Mr. Stevenson,

Several associates have mentioned the quality of your search
work for managers in this area. Peter Spina was particularly
complimentary. I think we should get to know one another.

My experience and track record in sales and marketing have been
excellent. Here's a brief summary:

- I was promoted to national sales manager after only two years
  with the firm and effected a 10% increase in market share for
  all products; up to 20% for several products. My sales force
  was revitalized and motivated.

- I increased the profitability by reducing costly
  administrative procedures. By giving the sales people more
  authority, time-consuming tasks were removed from their agenda
  and they were able to do what they do best—sell.

- My track record with all the companies I have been with from
  salesman to national sales manager are all positive—all have
  shown increased sales.

My career has been good but our president has reluctantly agreed
with me that to optimize my career possibilities, I should look
to a larger organization.

Please call me at your convenience. I have given my secretary
your name.

Sincerely,

Wesley A. Glaves

78 Library Lane
Atherton CA 94025
415-555-2697

Dear Sir or Madam:

I am writing to you in response to your advertisement for a Research Manager/Analyst in the San Francisco Examiner. I am currently working in a capacity similar to the one which you so described and would like to be considered for the position.

Since graduating from the University of San Francisco with a B.S. degree in marketing, I have been employed as a marketing analyst for Market Trend Analysts, Inc., a market research firm that produces and sells business information reports. In my current capacity as project director, it is my responsibility to:

- Research and analyze the past performance of various industries, in order to project future growth.

- Write press releases and direct mail marketing brochures.

- Coordinate the activities of research assistants assigned to my projects.

Samples of these reports will be available for inspection at any subsequent interview.

As an Honors student, I was exposed to a curriculum that effectively blended solid business courses with advanced liberal arts courses. As a result, I have come away from this experience with a well-rounded, liberal education that is considerate, not only of the business aspect of life, but of the human aspect as well. While writing my Honors Thesis, "Developing Cost-Effective Advertising Campaigns," I performed independent research on: Product Positioning,

Creative Techniques, Media Planning, and Campaign Coordination. A copy of my thesis will also be available for inspection at these subsequent interviews. My grades in all areas were excellent.

Prior to attending college, I held a supervisory position at Uni-Research, a subsidiary of Big-Time Publishing located in Redwood City. There I demonstrated the ability to analyze situations in a manner that facilitated problem solving and problem prevention. I proved to be an excellent motivator and had an outstanding rapport with those inside and outside of my department. I have worked with personal computers and mainframes both professionally and educationally.

Please review the enclosed resume and transcripts. I feel I am well equipped to satisfy the needs of this position and would appreciate the opportunity to be interviewed at any time that is convenient to you.

Sincerely,

Cliff Peterson

4545 Peachtree Lane, NE
Atlanta, GA 30317
404-555-7856

Accounting Manager Position
Box 3454
Atlanta Constitution
Atlanta, GA 30317

To Whom It May Concern:

I am interested in applying for the position of Accounting Manager that was advertised in the Atlanta Constitution.

I have worked at my present job for the last five years and it's time for me to move on and better myself. I like the paper business and am looking for more responsibility and challenges in a new position.

As you will note from the enclosed resume, I have thirteen years of varied accounting experience in which I have acquired and refined the following strengths:

• Strength in planning, control and responsibility reporting, especially in regard to costing nonmanufacturing activities and the use of the contribution approach in costing.

• Varied background in inventory planning, control, and valuation.

• Superior job costing and manufacturing overhead and cost allocation skills.

• Knowledge of the importance of proper accounting procedures for an organization.

I offer your company substantial experience and the high degree of excellence needed to produce quality financial reports. I look forward to getting together to discuss how my services and expertise can match your needs.

Cordially,

Richard Rollins

Letter that Highlights

○ Good highlighting
○ Not as well targeted as it could be; this was not a blind-box ad, so applicant could have found name of employer
○ Request for interview is very wishy-washy
○ Grade: B

1 Patrick Court
Southbury, CT 06488
203-555-1111

Photographer Position
Associated Press
125 E. 43rd Street
New York, NY 10017

Dear Ms./Mr.:

As an experienced and professional photographer, I would welcome the opportunity to discuss my qualifications for the position advertised in The New York Times. I am familiar with all phases of photography, including darkroom procedures.

• At present, I am a stringer for both AP and UPI wire services.

• For the past year, I have been darkroom supervisor at one of the largest commercial darkrooms in Connecticut, where I developed a procedure that reduces the amount of downtime in the developing process, thus saving the company thousands of dollars.

• I have been a professional photographer for more than five years, and have shot all kinds of work: news, features, social, studio and underwater.

I would be most interested in discussing the full-time position advertised, as well as the possibility of being associated with your firm as a freelance stringer.

If you believe a personal interview would prove worthwhile, please phone me at my Connecticut residence (203) 555-1111. I would be most interested in the possibility of letting you examine my extensive portfolio. I look forward to hearing from you.

Sincerely,

Carolyn Papery

Letter that Highlights

○ Good highlighting
○ Biggest problem is sexist salutation
○ Leaves ball in employer's court
○ Grade: B+

1050 Wilshire Blvd.,
#234
Los Angeles, CA 91440
818-555-1050

Gentlemen:

Enclosed please find my resume in response to your ad in this Sunday's Los Angeles Times for a Biotechnology Project Manager. This position is very much in line with my present career objective, and I believe my professional qualifications are very much in line with your requirements.

Consider the following professional highlights:

— More than 10 years of in-depth biotechnological experience in a variety of settings.

— Solid, hands-on proficiency with a wide range of biotechnological techniques.

— Played a vital role on team that developed a hybridoma, a cell created by fusing a human cancer cell with a white blood cell.

— Worked with Dr. Ananda Chakrabarty of the University of Illinois (while getting my doctorate) on gene splicing experiments that produced a strain of bacteria that eats oil spills.

I would welcome the opportunity for a personal interview to further discuss your requirements. I can be reached at (818) 555-1050.

Thank you for your consideration, and I look forward to hearing from you.

Sincerely,

Nick Birdman

○ Quote and its attribution take up so much space
   that there is room for little else.
○ Grade: C

450 Market St., Apt. 1A
San Francisco, CA 94102
315-555-4321

Dear Friends,

What is a Good Bookseller?

To be a successful bookseller, one needs an
innate fondness for books, an infinite capacity for
pains in handling details, a certain poise and
self-confidence, which is the basis of selling
ability. Beyond these, one must cultivate business
ability, for successful bookstore management is based
fundamentally on the same principles as any other
retail business: aggressive merchandising and sound
financial control.

—Frederick G. Melcher
The Successful Bookshop
(New York: National Association of Book
Publishers, 1926) quoted in A Manual on
Bookselling

I'm extremely interested in making a contribution to your bookstore
chain, and I believe I embody the qualities in Melcher's quote.
There are several B. Dalton stores here in the San Francisco area,
including the brand new store on Market Street.

Although I have been in publishing and printing for the past few
years, I have been looking for a good opportunity to get back into
the retail book business, preferably at the management level. I
have extensive bookstore experience, as well as a general
retail/customer service background.

I know I could add to the success of the B. Dalton chain. I will
call you next week to discuss the possibility of an interview.
Thank you kindly for your time and consideration.

Sincerely,

Steve Spurt

Clever Angle Letter

○ Beginning takes too long to get to the point
○ Seems more interested in what the company can do
   for him than what he can do for company
○ Grade: C

26 Windover Way
Portland, ME 04107
207-555-2626

Mr. Steven Davis
Wang Laboratories
100 Route 2A
Boston, MA 02143

Dear Mr. Davis,

In the chronology of computers, starting in the 1940s with the
development of the first general purpose digital computer through
the 1950s and the development of UNIVACs through the 1960s and the
development of COBOL through the 1970s and the development of
fourth-generation integrated circuits through the 1980s and the
development of Macintosh computers to the 1990s and beyond and the
development of Next computers and artificial intelligence, you and
your companies have been significant players in the development of
computers and the "computer age."

I am writing to you because my main objective as a computer
programmer is to associate with a firm that is truly in the
mainstream of computer technology.

At present, as you will note in the enclosed resume, I am
associated with Futuristic Computers, Inc., as a senior designer
and programmer. This position affords me very heavy experience in
all phases of hardware and software development.

Futuristic Computers is highly satisfied with my services, but I
feel I would be much happier working for a mainstream computer
company, where my experience and expertise can be used to advance
the computer age—and to help continue you and your company's
reputation as the future of computers.

May I meet with you sometime soon and discuss more fully my desire
to become associated with you and your company? It would be most
rewarding and satisfying to work for a company so involved in the
evolution of computers.

Sincerely yours,

Andrew Williams

Clever Angle Letter

❍ Takes a long time to get to the point
❍ Long, with some unnecessary details and negative information
❍ Too much emphasis on academic frame of reference
❍ Demonstrates excellent knowledge of recipient's work
❍ Grade: B

936A S.W. 2nd Avenue
Gainesville, FL 32601
904-555-1234

Dear Mr. Rudolph,

Space, and the handling of it psychologically, is something that you and I have in common. Psychology is the basis for my master's thesis, which I have been reading toward these past six years while in school.

This is something that I have noticed has existed in your work since I've been aware of you. You confirmed and explained further these attitudes toward architecture in your lecture here at the University of Florida. I've been watching your work closely for over seven years.

My work has taken a direction that has a fluidity which is similar to the grand stair of your Health, Welfare and Education Service Center, Boston 1970. I still believe in the straight line though I find it most often submissive to the curve. The flowing form, I believe, is most appropriate to human movement and movement of vision.

My thesis "Motion Through Architecture," now in the works, is nearing completion. I should be meeting all requirements for my Master's of Art in Architecture by June 15th. I would very much like to carry on the basis of the thesis in the climate of an office that would welcome it. My experience is, as you can see in my resume, limited. However my portfolios of both work and design will be much more impressive. With my past experience I have learned enough to know that I must work for an office that I can feel excited about. I believe your's would be just such an office.

I intend to be in New York June 25th through the 30th and already have an apartment in New York City. I would then like to ask for an appointment within the above dates to visit your office and speak with you personally in hopes to talk further with you in the direction your lecture took here.

I look forward to your favorable response.

Sincerely,

Wayne David

101 Franklin Blvd.
Summit, NJ 07901
201-555-1010

Mr. Jim Goudy
First Jersey Insurance Co.
4567 Springfield Avenue
Newark, NJ 07105

Dear Mr. Goudy,

According to the local newspaper, there were more than 200 "suspicious" fires in Newark in 1987. Of those 200+ fires, only about 20 were ever officially logged as arson. That's less than a 10% success ratio.

My 15 years as a fire marshall with the Newark Fire Department and my seven years as fire investigator with Mid-Atlantic Insurance Company, Inc.—where my arson success ratio is close to 50%, should qualify me for the position of Chief Fire Investigator.

My work with the arson squad of the Newark Fire Department earned high praise and three citations from the mayor's office. My work with Mid-Atlantic has saved the company millions of dollars in fraudulent fire claims.

Although I am happy in my present job and Mid-Atlantic is certainly more than satisfied with my work, I feel it's time to move from being an indian to becoming a chief, where with my keen sense of investigating, I can lead a team and help your company save millions of dollars.

I would like to discuss my qualifications more fully with you in the near future. I will call you next Tuesday to see if we can find an agreeable time.

Thank you for your time and consideration.

Sincerely,

Dan Kostrinsky

Letter that Demonstrates Ideas

○ Breaks a cardinal rule by going to two pages
○ But makes up for it by great highlighting and
   demonstration of ideas
○ Resulted in an interview and job offer
○ Grade: A-

25 S.W. 95th Street
Belleview, FL 32620
904-555-9525

Vera A. Kingston
Marion County Newspapers, Inc.
P.O. Box 3232
Ocala, FL 32670

Dear Ms. Kingston,

I am writing to apply for the position of managing editor as
described in the March 5th Marion Journal.

My background and skills include:

• One year in the position of staff writer for the West Palm
  Reader, West Palm Beach, Florida. In that capacity I covered
  and reported on school board meetings, selection meetings and
  Town Meetings. From these meetings I identified and reported
  on additional news and feature stories. I also interviewed
  prominent citizens and reviewed school productions.

• I have considerable additional writing experience gained from
  over twelve years experience in the insurance field. In that
  capacity I wrote reports and instructional/training manuals.

• I have a great deal of management and staff assignments
  experience achieved through both my insurance work and
  managing my own consulting practice from 1980 to 1988.

Some of my ideas for a town newspaper include:

• Extensive coverage of town civic and municipal meetings along
  with pertinent feature articles and interviews

• Extensive coverage of school events. Inclusion of school news
  and students' names frequently boosts resident interest in
  issues and increases circulation. This could possibly include
  a high school student to write a regular school news column.
  Personal contact with each school's principal would facilitate
  this process.

• "Person on the street" responses to town-related issues;

Vera A. Kingston   -2-

- Candidate responses to pre-determined questions to allow for easier citizen evaluation of candidates and their positions;

- Review of local events in the style of theater critical reviews, again including names and pictures;

- A regular column highlighting a local activity or nearby historical site. The column would not only include basic description of the activity but pertinent information of interest to parents. For example: For what age children is the activity appropriate? Strollers or backpackers? Are facilities available for diaper change? Kinds and costs of snacks available? Are picnic facilities available? How long should a visit take? Does use of the facility vary seasonally? Etc. A column such as this would not only highlight a current event but would increase resident awareness of Florida resources.

I would be very interested in discussing this position with you.

Sincerely,

Shari Thomann

Cold Contact Letter

- ○ Does good job of praising employer in first line
- ○ She's otherwise not able to build a very strong case on the basis of one news release
- ○ Grade: C

5603 Main Street
Detroit, MI 48201
313-555-1333

Mr. Rudolph S. Hearst
Detroit Daily News
News Building
Detroit, MI 48201

Dear Mr. Hearst,

I am impressed by the way you present the news to the community and I would like to work for your company.

I'm sure you know, from the News Release I sent you on December 18, 1988, that my company, Ancient Automotive, Inc., is closing its doors and I, the executive word-processing secretary for the marketing communications department with 10 years experience, will be seeking employment very shortly.

My responsibilities include complete coordination of News Releases. A copy of a news release which I was instrumental in releasing to the media is attached along with my resume for your review and consideration.

I am looking forward to hearing from you.

Sincerely yours,

Fannie Maye

Cold Contact Letter

○ Takes direct, active approach to requesting an interview
○ A little skimpy on detail as applied to position
○ Grade: B+

834 Main Street
Stillwater, OK 74074
405-555-4545

Ms. Devon Jones
Able Consulting Partners, Inc.
23 Mountain Pass
Stillwater, OK 74074

Dear Ms. Jones,

I'd like to talk to you about the possibility of a staff position with your consulting company.

Enclosed are a resume and a list of accomplishments for your review. You will see that I have a varied and strong business background which you would find useful. After some time out of school and agency work, I have decided to pursue a career in business and marketing.

Although I have been accepted as a graduate assistant at the University of Oklahoma, I would rather start working right away. I believe I have the skills to be an asset to you now. Perhaps you could use me for freelance work.

I will call you next week to see if you wish to arrange an interview. Thank you for considering my resume, and I look forward to meeting with you.

Sincerely,

Alice Love

○ Good trumpeting of accomplishments
○ Good, proactive approach to interview
○ A little long
○ Grade: A-

19 Berkley Street
Maplewood, NJ 07040
201-555-1212

Dr. Julius Kane
Syracuse Law Partners
50 Comstock Blvd.
Syracuse, NY 13215

Dear Dr. Kane,

My recent experience as director of public information at an All National Law Clinic and my commitment to legal issues would enable me to make a significant contribution in a public relations/public affairs/community relations capacity. I will be relocating to Syracuse within a year because my husband has just accepted an offer to teach at Syracuse University.

Among the highlights of my tenure at All Nation has been the launch of a new clinic site. I developed a very successful marketing plan within tight budget restrictions, and as a result, the new clinic is not only building its caseload with each passing week, but we have also generated excellent awareness and enthusiasm for our services.

When I leave All Nation next year, I will have three newsletters and two annual reports under my belt. The publications I've produced thus far have been extremely well received.

I've also developed an aggressive program of regular press releases, having learned a great deal about how to get releases into print from my years as an editor. I have an excellent record of getting releases placed in local publications.

I will relocate to Syracuse no later than August, 1990, but I could relocate sooner should you have an appropriate opening. I would be willing to fly up for an interview at virtually any time, and it is likely I will be in Upstate New York around Christmastime. I will call you then to see if we can set up an exploratory interview even if you have no openings.

Should you wish to reach me to set up an interview, you may leave a message at 201-555-1212, or call that number after business hours or call me at All Nation at 201-555-9999. I'm sure my executive director would give me a fine recommendation, however, he doesn't know I'm leaving yet, so I would appreciate your discretion.

Cordially,

Joan E. Dreskin

Cold Contact Letter

- Quantifies accomplishments
- Does an excellent job of telling what he can do for the company and its profitability
- Loses impact with passive closing
- Grade: A-

RR Box 12
Waverly, VT 05492
802-555-5555

Dear Mr. Black,

More than three years ago, I left the Philadelphia area to receive a working education in media and media sales. My resume indicates that I have not only learned my business from a variety of angles, but also quickly progressed to a position of responsibility in every company.

Each promotion was based on my aggressiveness and a well-proven ability to make money. I can now do the same for your company.

In my most recent position, I took a department that was already 6% behind established goals. Within a six month period, I had completely reversed that figure—plus.

The enclosed resume only partially reveals my qualities as an advertising executive and idea man. I am experienced in many facets of marketing, budget and profit planning. I have much experience in general management planning and have proven quite capable of turning a disorganized and unprofitable crew into a well-run and money-making machine.

I am currently planning to return to the Philadelphia area to put my experience to work. After two harsh Vermont winters, I am ready to return to my old stomping grounds as soon as possible.

I hope to hear from you shortly and would be happy to travel to your area anytime for an interview. Thank you for your consideration of me.

Sincerely,

John Smith

Cold Contact Letter

- ○ Does a good job of telling what the applicant can do for the company
- ○ Good highlighting
- ○ Drops the ball by not taking proactive approach to interview
- ○ Grade: A-

85 W. 78th Street
New York, NY 10023
212-555-1010

Ms. Vanessa Graham
City Medical Supplies
23 Houston Street
New York, NY 10005

Dear Ms. Graham,

In my four years as sales manager of a leading medical supplies distributor in Westchester County, I directed the sales and marketing policies of the company's line of medical supplies and accessories.

During that time:

- — Annual billings more than tripled from $3.25 million to $10.75 million.

- — Profits rose five-fold, from $150,000 in 1984 to $785,000 for the fiscal year ending September, 1988.

- — Number of accounts within same geographical territory increased by more than 250%.

The success I've had here and elsewhere in 12 years of selling is not a coincidence, or attributable to luck or magic. My sales success is due in part to my education in Business Administration (Harvard, 1976) and a natural ability to analyze a marketing/selling situation and come up with an innovative program that leaves the competition way behind.

What I have done for my previous employers, I am confident I can do for you.

I would be glad to make myself available for a personal interview where we can discuss how I can serve your company in increasing sales and market share.

Sincerely yours,

Thomas Mahoney

Cold Contact Letter

- Good use of "what I can do for the company"
- The only things that could make this letter better are a little pizazz and more specific reference to the company
- Grade: A

209F N.W. 111th Street
Gainesville, FL 32609
904-555-5665

Mr. David Heller
N.J. Research, Inc.
34 Consultants Court
Princeton, NJ 08540

Dear Mr. Heller,

As marketing research companies are increasingly called upon to supply information on magazine readership to publishers, there is a growing need for trained and experienced professionals in the field.

Through my marketing/research experience and my master's thesis, which have particularly dealt with improving marketing readership studies so they can better define magazine audiences to potential advertisers, I am certain I could give you valuable assistance in satisfying research demands and improving the marketing tools you currently use.

I will be completing my master's degree in December and would be interested in making a contribution to N.J. Research's profitability in a marketing/research capacity.

I believe my services would be useful to you, and I will call you in late September to discuss an interview. Thank you for your time and consideration.

Sincerely,

Scott Morris

Classified Ad Response Letter

- ❍ Too short
- ❍ Says he has experience directly related to specifications, but doesn't describe it
- ❍ Clearly, applicant writes the same letter to all ads
- ❍ Sexist salutation
- ❍ Grade: D

23 Rockefeller Circle
Great Neck, NY 11021
914-555-2323

The Reknown School of Music
10 Park Avenue
New York, NY 10001

Gentlemen:

Please accept my resume for consideration for the position of Music Director with your school.

I have an extensive background in music, and experience directly related to the job specifications noted in the Sunday's Times advertisement.

I may be reached at the above number.

Thank you.

Cordially,

Brad Bayne

```
                                     65 Pontiac Drive
                                     Detroit, MI 48222
                                     313-555-3333

Big Bend Automotive, Inc.
23 Ann Arbor Beltway
Detroit, MI 48222

To Whom It May Concern,

I have recently been laid off from the Greenwood Parts
Company, a subsidiary of Big Three Automotive, Inc., and I
am responding to your advertisement soliciting
applications from automotive parts inventory clerks.

My background is quite extensive and can be of great value
to your organization. The combination of my knowledge of
automotive parts and my skills of inventory control make
me a perfect fit for your opening.

In terms of salary requirements, I expect fair and
competitive compensation.

Thank you for your interest. I look forward to hearing
from you soon.

Sincerely,


Donald A. Gone
```

70

Classified Ad Response Letter

○ Cliche-laden
○ Too short and sketchy. He should spell out how his training and experience run parallel to the demands of the position.
○ He shouldn't list references until interview stage
○ Grade: C

Tobacco Processing Manager
Career opportunity in major food diversified company for a tobacco processing manager. Must have experience in food tobacco processing and some supervisory experience helpful. Write to Adam Jones, Box 112, News-Beacon.

2513 Green Leaves
Avenue
Winston-Salem, NC
27105
919-555-9911

Dear Mr. Jones,

In response to your ad in the Sunday, January 4 issue of the Winston-Salem News-Beacon, I am taking the liberty of forwarding a personal resume touching upon certain aspects of my technical and supervisory background which should prove to be of interest to you and your company at this time.

As you will note, my entire educational history and work experience in tobacco processing run parallel to the demands of the position you advertise.

I am presently employed as Tobacco Inspection Supervisor with American Brands, 21943 U.S. Highway 89, Winston-Salem, N.C. For reference, you may contact my supervisor, Mr. Thomas Holton, who I have made aware of my intention of seeking employment outside the company.

I will be glad to make myself available for an interview at any time to your convenience.

Sincerely yours,

Glen C. Voe

Classified Ad Response Letter

- If she knows enough about the firm to say she's interested in working there, she could have found out the name of personnel director and could have taken a proactive approach to asking for an interview
- Sketchy; doesn't apply experience to the position
- Grade: C

55 Hickory Hill
Lincoln, MA 01773
617-555-4334

Personnel Director
Massachusetts Computers, Inc.
234 Boylston Street
Boston, MA 02138

Dear Personnel Director,

Having read your advertisement in Sunday's Boston Globe, I believe I am a qualified candidate for a position in your firm. I am interested in your firm because I feel I have so much to offer.

Presently I am working for Intercounty Office Machines in Brookline. I am seeking a career change into computers. My degree is in computer science with a minor in mathematics. My knowledge of computers ranges from mainframes to personal computers.

I have enclosed a resume listing further qualifications. Thank you for taking the time to consider my resume and I would appreciate the opportunity of a personal interview. I can be reached at 617-555-4334 and look forward to hearing from you.

Sincerely,

Stephanie Digitali

Classified Ad Response Letter

❍ A decent letter that falls down several notches by inserting negative information that could just as easily have been left out
❍ Leaves ball in employer's court
❍ Grade: C

13 Greenfield Place
Trenton, NJ 08608
609-555-9999

Ms. Shelly Hass
Trenton Museum
23 Museum Court
Trenton, NJ 08608

Dear Ms. Hass,

I would like to apply for the assistant curator position your museum advertised in the Sunday, August 12 edition of the Trenton Times.

From my resume, you will see that I minored in art history and have experience in working with art. In my last job, which I lost due to personnel cutbacks, I was responsible for everything from cataloging new works of art to assisting designing exhibits.

I have also held several positions of leadership that required extensive use of my organizational and people skills.

In addition, I would like to add that I am a fast learner and a hard, enthusiastic worker.

Thank you in advance for your time and consideration. I would appreciate the opportunity to meet with you to discuss how I might be of service to your organization. If you have any further questions about my qualifications, please contact me at the above telephone number.

Sincerely yours,

Charles A. Brown

- ○ Improper salutation
- ○ Decent knowledge about company and position
- ○ Leans toward "what you can do for me"
- ○ Leaves ball in employer's court
- ○ Grade: C+

98 Okayeebee Street
Wabash, IN 46992
219-555-2121

Ms. Mary D. Donahue
General Foods
10 Delbarton Drive
Indianapolis, IN 46201

Dear Mary,

Currently employed as administrative assistant to one of my company's vice presidents, I am seeking employment where my secretarial, administrative and management background can be better utilized.

Having graduated from the University of Indiana in June, I believe my comprehensive relative experience and interpersonal contact I gained through extracurricular and summer job involvement has prepared me extremely well for an executive administrator career.

Since I have been a consumer of General Foods for as long as I can recall, this particular opening with the executive vice president is of special importance in fulfilling my desires.

The enclosed resume provides specific information concerning my academic background and activities encountered in college.

I am very enthusiastic about exploring my candidacy for this position. I would appreciate the opportunity of an interview. I can be reached at (219) 555-2121 after 6 p.m. or you can call me during business hours at (219) 555-4343. I look forward to hearing from you.

Sincerely,

Nancy C. Rider

○ Uses "clever angle" beginning, which takes a little
   too long to get to the point
○ The information about the lack of a degree, though
   well-expressed, is unnecessary
○ Grade: B

EDITORIAL
Career-minded, goal-oriented editorial staffer with Journalism or related degree. Experience necessary but achievers eager to learn & willing to work hard will also be considered. Reply to 1939 INQUIRER.

100A East Oceanview Drive
Peahala Park, NJ 08008
609-555-6969

Dear Friends,

I once read a checklist designed to help a person determine if he or she would be suited for a career in publishing. "Do you hang out in bookstores and newsstands?," it read, "Do you spot typos whenever you read anything? Are you a good organizer and compulsive about detail? Do you have a good memory? Can you juggle many projects simultaneously and still meet deadlines? Are you into producing newsletters and/or did you work for your college paper?"

And I thought, "Good heavens, they've been following me around." The description does seem tailor-made for me.

If you are willing to consider a hard-working, eager-to-learn degreed but inexperienced person for your editorial staff, will you also consider someone with the same qualities and great experience but less than four years of college? I mention my lack of degree so I won't waste anyone's time, but I sincerely believe my experience is worth its weight in sheepskin any day.

I'm a highly motivated, energetic, well-organized self-starter, as demonstrated by my former employers who have recognized my achievements and rapidly promoted me to positions of greater responsibility. I absolutely thrive on pressure and have no qualms whatsoever about hard work because I love this field.

I have recently returned to my native Philadelphia area after two years in Tennessee as editor of a new city magazine in Knoxville. In my effort to learn the publishing business from every angle. I've been working as a traffic manager at Lewis & Gilman, Philadelphia's largest ad agency. Here, I've made good use of my organizational talent in overseeing the production of ads from conception to publication. I would, however, prefer to be closer to my beloved publishing field.

I would be most happy to make myself available for an interview at your convenience. During business hours, I can be reached at 215-555-3775, extension 386. Thanking you most kindly for your consideration of me, I look forward to hearing from you.

Cordially,

Kate Sumner

20 Ewing Court
Dallas, TX 75228
214-555-2222

Kay Johnston
Dallas Morning Star
Morning Star Blvd.
Dallas, TX 75228

Dear Kay,

This is in response to the Morning-Star 8/12 advertisement for an editorial cartoonist. Please consider my qualifications:

* I created a weekly editorial comic strip that was published by nearly 50 newspapers in Texas.

* The comic strip won several awards, including the Texas Society of Professional Journalists coveted Editorial Cartoon of the year.

* Topics covered by the strip were always timely and relevant, covering a wide variety of national and local issues, from President Reagan to the collapse of savings and loans in Texas.

* I did all this on a part-time basis while completing a full load of classes to finish course requirements for a master's in political science at the University of Texas-Dallas. I also completed courses in journalism and art.

* In addition to my weekly strip, I worked one summer as a staff artist for the Dallas Beacon.

* Before working toward the master's degree, I earned a B.A. at UT-Austin in fine arts.

Please contact me for an interview.

Yours truly,

Robert Duffy

Classified Ad Response Letter

○ Good letter; a little long
○ Should take proactive stance with interview request
○ Grade: A-

110 Ocean Blvd.
Los Angeles, CA 90005
213-555-5678

Dear Dr. Davis,

The most important criteria in a professor are professional experience, teaching ability, and research potential. With my marketing and management experience as well as my college teaching experience, I would like to be considered for a position as one of your entry-level assistant professors. I feel confident that I am strongly qualified—and—I would love to teach any and all of the courses you mentioned in your ad in the Marketing News.

I would bring the strength of several years in the marketing field, a BS in marketing from Syracuse University and an MBA with a concentration in marketing from New York University, as well as the years of experience teaching both large and small classes.

I am especially strong in marketing research—both qualitative and quantitative, and am well versed in all aspects of promotion, advertising, consumer behavior, and marketing and business management.

My teaching skills are excellent. I am always evaluated highly by my students and department heads. I enjoy the interaction with students and am comfortable with both large lecture classes as well as smaller groups.

Please look over the enclosed resume and list of courses I have taught, and I believe you will find a strong candidate for the position.

I look forward to hearing from you in the near future. Please call me if there is anything else you might need, or if you have any questions. Enclosed, as the ad requested, you will find my vita, listing of courses taught, and the names of three references.

Thank you for your valuable time and consideration.

Sincerely,

Peter Kiser

10 Redwood Forest Lane
Sacramento, CA 95841
916-555-1010

Mr. Jeff Green
The Health Center
45 Medical Court
Sacramento, CA 95841

Dear Jeff Green,

My strong writing background and intense interest in health care would enable me to make a significant contribution to the media information director position you are currently advertising.

I'm a competent, award-winning writer and editor. One of the pieces I've won awards for is a weekly column that has dealt exclusively with social, family and health issues. I have enclosed writing samples that show my commitment to health care issues.

I'm available immediately to help meet your writing and placement needs. I have good contacts in the media.

My respect and admiration for The Health Center goes a back a long way. I came to you for my health-care needs as a teenager, and I have relied on you for care and information ever since. I am truly committed to your mission.

I can make myself available for an interview at your convenience. Thanking you most kindly for your consideration, I look forward to meeting with you soon.

Cordially,

Debbie Bayne

Classified Ad Response Letter

○ Provides enticement for employer to call by offering to show clips, but still leaves ball in employer's court
○ Grade: A-

1090 Peachtree Lane, #23
Atlanta, GA 30303
404-555-4040

Ms. Judy Sumner
The Atlanta Constitution
Constitution Court
Atlanta, GA 30303

Dear Ms. Sumner,

I have the skills and potential to fill the editorial position you advertised for in the August 10, 1989 newspaper.

Until I moved, I was a reporter for the Chattanooga News-Free Press (circulation 100,000). Working general assignments on the city side, I covered stories on all available beats; politics, city and county courts, education, police and fire, business and religion. I also wrote weekly Sunday features and occasional sports stories and restaurant reviews.

Under a veteran city editor who believes in exposing his staff to varied experiences, I had an opportunity to do layout, write headlines and edit copy.

While at the University of Tennessee at Chattanooga, I worked for four years on the university newspaper and was assistant editor of the campus literary magazine. An English major, I graduated magna cum laude.

My enclosed resume contains information on my previous work experience and successful academic career. I have also enclosed recommendations from several editors on our staff.

I would like to show you my strong collection of clips and can be contacted for an interview at 404-555-4040. I will look forward to hearing from you.

Sincerely,

Wesley D. Captain

Classified Ad Response Letter

- Speaks well to requirements expressed in ad
- Resulted in an interview
- Information about why she left her last job could have been left out
- Leaves ball in employer's court
- Grade: A-

9020 Walker Driver
Chapel Hill, NC 27514
919-555-1515

Dear Mr. Squirrel,

My experience as a creative assignment editor and my supervisory background would enable me to make a significant contribution to the assistant metro editor position you are currently advertising.

Most recently, I was executive editor of a group of 10 weekly newspapers in Austin County. I left there to help my husband launch a new business, but now that he's on the verge of landing his first major account, I'm eager to get back into newspapers. Before my last job, I was city editor at the daily in Texas' third-largest city.

A real strength of mine is story ideas. I'm able to ensure my reporters never miss what they should be covering, but I can often suggest an unusual approach that puts the story into perspective for readers.

And once the copy is in, I get great satisfaction from working with the reporter to mold it into the clear, crisp, concise piece of prose it should be.

One of my proudest editing achievements along these lines was at a daily in Florida, where a story I conceived, assigned and edited went on to win the national Rolling Stone entertainment writing award for 1984.

At The Austin News-Beacon, I consistently showed superior news judgment in pitching stories on the daily news budget and in the news meeting. That's why I was promoted from assistant city editor to city editor after only three months.

I can make myself available for an interview at your convenience and can be reached during business hours at 919-555-9876.

Thanking you most kindly for your consideration of me, I look forward to meeting with you soon.

Sincerely,

Theresa Simmons

Classified Ad Response Letter

❍ Terrific approach to speaking to requirements of the ad
❍ Assertive request for interview but still leaves ball in employer's court
❍ Grade: A-

7 Wipper Court
Beaver Falls, PA 15010
412-555-7777

Mr. Jack C. Able
Personnel Director
Xerox Corp.
1238 Bayshore Court
Stamford, CT 06900

Dear Mr. Able:

Your advertisement in today's Wall Street Journal stimulated my interest and seems to match exactly my particular background and skills.

You Require:	My Qualifications:
Advanced Degree	I have an MBA from the Wharton School, specializing in accounting
10 years accounting experience in large corporate environment	4 years, Accountant at E.F. Hutton
	3 years, Senior Accountant at American Express
	4 years, Manager of Accounts, Exxon Corp.
EDP applications	Designed integrated EDP invoicing system for American Express. IBM, Digital, mainframe experience.

Since my experience and knowledge fit your requirements exactly, I am clearly one of the people you'll want to see. Please call me at my home number only. I look forward to our meeting.

Sincerely,

Warren D. Nissani

Classified Ad Response Letter

- ○ Does a good job of speaking to the requirements of the ad
- ○ Conveys warmth and enthusiasm
- ○ Uses appealing empathic approach to interview request and also takes initiative
- ○ Grade: A

2332 Alpine Drive
Denver, CO 80210
303-555-2332

Ms. Amber Aspen
Denver Board of Education
75 Mountain Lakes Drive
Denver, CO 80210

Dear Ms. Aspen,

Perhaps I am the "multi-talented teacher" you seek in your "Multi-Talented Teacher" advertisement in today's Denver Post. I'm a versatile teacher, ready to substitute, if necessary, as early as next week. I have the solid teaching experience you specify.

As you will note on the enclosed resume, I am presently affiliated with a highly regarded private elementary school. Mr. Vail, the headmaster, will certainly give you a good reference. The details of your advertisement suggest to me that the position will involve many of the same responsibilities that I am currently performing.

In addition to the planning, administration, and student-parent counseling duties I highlight in my resume, please note that I have a master's degree as well as a teaching certificate from the state of Colorado.

Knowing how frantic you must be without an a fifth grade teacher, I will call you in a few days. Or if you agree upon reviewing my letter and resume that I am the teacher you need, call me at the home number listed above or at 555-1101 during business hours.

Thanking you most sincerely for your time and consideration.

Cordially,

Maria Plazza

Classified Ad Response Letter

- A nice, concise letter that tells in a few well-chosen words what applicant can do for company
- Takes proactive approach to interview request
- Grade: A

1200 Lake Shore Avenue
Chicago, IL 60606
312-555-5555

Mr. Horace Pass
General Food Corp.
200 Wacker Drive
Chicago, IL 60606

Dear Mr. Pass,

Your display ad in last Sunday's Tribune for a Brand Manager for a major packaged goods product is of special interest to me because it calls for qualifications which completely correspond to my background and job objective.

As you can see on my resume, in addition to an excellent professional background in brand management, I have had particular success with new product introductions, twice being promoted because of my ideas and innovations.

It is time for me to move on to a company such as yours, which I know to be one of the largest and most prestigious food companies in the United States. I have had seven solid years of experience on a smaller scale and now want to bring my ideas and knowledge to your firm.

May I ask you to read the resume and permit me to phone your secretary next week for an appointment? I look forward to meeting you and thank you for your time and consideration.

Sincerely,

Gretchen Tisch

Blind Box Ad Response Letter

- O Too short; a cover letter like this is tantamount to no cover letter at all
- O Expects resume to do all the work
- O Does not ask for interview
- O Grade: D

10-40 Glass Street
Long Island City, NY
11111
718-555-3573

Polymer Chemist Position
Box 23
The American Chemist Journal
23 Brewer Drive
Milwaukee, WI 53219

To Whom It May Concern:

I am very interested in the position of polymer chemist, for which you advertised on September 25, in The American Chemist Journal. I feel that my qualifications, as detailed in the enclosed resume, make me an excellent candidate for this position. My current annual salary is $38,000.

Thank you for considering me for this position.

Sincerely yours,

Mitch R. Holms

Blind Box Ad Response Letter

- Leans too heavily toward the "What you can do for me" genre, although she does use the word "contribution."
- Grade: C+

102 East 95th Street
New York, NY 10128
212-555-9595

Box 112A
New York Times
New York, NY 10022

Dear Sir or Madam,

I am interested in the Research Analyst position you advertised for in The New York Times on Sunday, September 27.

As you can see from my resume, I have a strong business background. As a Product Analyst, I develop strategic business plans, analyze marketing proposals, make product management decisions, and implement presentations. As well as having excellent analytical skills, I am an extremely energetic and creative individual with a strong desire to work in a dynamic and challenging environment.

My experiences at Bankers Trust have been valuable because they have helped me to define my goals. I have researched many industries in which to continue my career, and I have found that Marketing is a terrific fit with my interests and personality. As a Research Analyst, I would be able to combine my insight and creativity with my marketing, organizational, and problem solving skills to make a unique contribution to your firm.

I am eager to speak with you about opportunities at your firm. I look forward to hearing from you soon.

Sincerely,

Jodi Welsh

919 Highpoint Ave., #33
Weehawken, NJ 07087
201-555-3333

To whom it may concern:

I am a research assistant at Ogilvy & Mather in New York, currently seeking employment elsewhere in a similar capacity. I'm very interested in the market research positions you have open.

In my time here, I developed a thorough knowledge of the IBM PC while working on new business as well as established accounts. I've demonstrated my ability to learn quickly and handle crises well, evident in the enclosed letters of recommendation.

Recently, my main responsibilities consisted of programming computer assisted telephone surveys and supervising a telephone interviewing unit of 4-6 people. I am familiar with the SAS and SPSS statistical analysis packages, Lotus 1-2-3, on-line research facilities such as IMS and Dialog and various word processing programs.

I would like to schedule an interview as soon as possible. Thank you very much for considering this application.

Sincerely,

Shari Thomann

200 River Road, Apt. 5C
Nutley, NJ 07110
201-555-2000

Box 234
Times
New York, NY 10017

Gentlemen:

Enclosed for your consideration is my resume, in response to your advertisement which appeared in The New York Times on October 25, 1989 for a market research manager.

I have extensive experience in the market research field on both the <u>client</u> side (with major packaged goods; HBA; consumer products, and electronics companies), as well as with several major <u>advertising agencies</u>. Additionally, as a consultant I gained invaluable experience working with market research <u>suppliers</u> on both qualitative and quantitative projects.

You will notice from my resume that I have worked on Widget Manufacturing's staff or served as a consultant to it over a period of years. Since discontinuing my relationship as of May, 1989, I am currently functioning as a freelance consultant but have an interest in returning to a full-time position within the industry. Please note that my resume provides a listing of some of my current freelance clients.

As a market research professional, my major accomplishments have been directed towards defining research problems and/or needs, devising appropriate techniques for their solution and resolving them through analytical marketing-oriented decisions.

I welcome the opportunity to discuss my resume and qualifications with you and to investigate any positions within your firm which are consistent with my background, salary requirements and career goals. If you wish to arrange an interview, I may be reach at (201) 555-2000.

Thanking you in advance for your consideration, I remain,

Cordially yours,

Matt Lastly

Blind Box Ad Response Letter

○ A bit long and unfocused; offers a menu of possibly relevant experience without honing in directly on USP. Admittedly, it may be hard to hone in when responding to a brief blind-box ad.

○ Grade: A-

3 Shetland Lane
Stamford, CT 06906
203-555-2323

To the PR/Ad Agency:

Researching a market and developing a working marketing and sales plan, producing creative and informative marketing/sales presentations, and communicating sales strategy to a target audience are just three of the skills I would bring to your agency as Ad Executive.

I have several years of key marketing, marketing research, copy writing, and promotion experience at some major publishing concerns, including Time, Inc.

I am currently Market Research Manager at Business Flyer magazine where my work has been focusing on the key marketing tools needed to relaunch the publication after years of stagnant inactivity—and these tools have worked, as the magazine is up sharply in ad pages and reader involvement.

I know that with my experience, my drive, and my abilities I can help your agency reach goals never obtained before.

Besides my strong advertising/marketing background, I can offer you someone who is an expert at desktop publishing. I am also currently president of my own consulting firm, and have clients such as Conde Nast, New York Times Company, the Stamford Journal, and others.

Besides this I am also an adjunct professor of business at Stamford Junior College, where I specialize in teaching advertising and marketing courses.

This is a major career move—both in terms of getting the opportunity to work on the agency side, and, geographically. But, as I grew up in Tampa, I have been waiting for the opportunity to return to Florida. I hope it is with the your agency.

I can make myself available for an interview at your convenience. I plan on relocating to Tallahassee in the near future, but can fly down for an interview at your convenience.

Sincerely,

Carol Ross

Blind Box Ad Response Letter

- ❍ Good use of Unique Selling Proposition
- ❍ Good use of broadcasting accomplishments
- ❍ Could have a more attention-grabbing beginning
- ❍ Grade: A-

101 Little Patuxent
Pkwy., #278
Columbia, MD 21044
301-555-5278

Dear Sir or Madam,

This letter is in response to your ad in The Sunday New York Times.

In my present position with Mason-Dixon Accounting, Inc., I further developed my management skills as well as a strong knowledge of financial accounting. Through the use of this knowledge and experience, I was able to greatly improve the manner in which financial accounting was conducted.

By devising and applying new systems, which utilized personnel and equipment more efficiently, I significantly reduced operating costs and time spent recording routine financial transactions. The end result was a more efficient organization offering higher quality financial accounting services.

I strongly feel that my experience and enthusiasm for doing quality financial accounting would be a good addition to your organization. I look forward to your response and the opportunity to further discuss the possibility of working for your company.

Sincerely,

Patty DeRoy

Blind Box Ad Response Letter

○ Applicant uses "contribution" to tell what she can do for employer
○ The "30-gallon trash can" phrase was popular with employers
○ Grade: A

29 Ocean Blvd.
Toms River, NJ 08753
609-555-9696

Dear Boxholder,

My strong writing background and keen interest in economic development would enable me to make a significant contribution to the public relations position you are currently advertising.

In my most recent editing positions, a 30-gallon trash can was the destination of 90 percent of the press releases I received. Based on seeing so many poorly written and mistargeted releases, I feel I could write a book or teach a course on how not to write a press release or run a publicity campaign.

I know what editors are looking for.

I know because I was most recently editor of 10 weekly papers in Ocean County. Before that, I was city editor at the newspaper in New Jersey's third-largest city. It's because of my inside knowledge of what drives editors crazy about public relations that I feel my experience is transferable to this slight shift in careers.

I'm a competent, award-winning writer and editor. One of the pieces I've won awards for is a weekly column that has dealt exclusively with social and family issues. I'm available immediately to help meet your writing and placement needs.

I can make myself available for an interview at your convenience and may be reached during business hours at 201-555-9528.

Thanking you most kindly for your consideration, I look forward to meeting with you soon.

Cordially,

Deirdre Cosgrove

Blind Box Ad Response Letter

○ Good job of highlighting accomplishments
○ Grade: A

91 Maple Street
Maplewood, NJ 07040
201-555-5555

Box 1543
New York Times
New York, NY 10022

Dear Boxholder,

My strong print production and exceptional organizational skills would enable me to make a significant contribution to the production editor position you are currently advertising.

Among my proudest accomplishments in my most recent position:

— When I arrived, no one in the editorial department knew what deadlines were or how to meet them. I set up policies and procedures that enabled the company to save all the money it had been throwing away on lost press time.

— I recently oversaw the transition from an old typesetting system to a state-of-the-art system. The transitions went more smoothly than anyone expected.

There is very little I don't know about print production, including four-color, imposition, and dummying. I have extensive experience in working with suppliers and coaxing the best from them under tough deadlines.

My facility with trafficking comes from working both in an advertising production capacity in magazine publishing and as a traffic manager at Chicago's largest ad agency.

I'm addicted to word processing and am adept at most computerized-typesetting, word-processing and desktop-publishing systems.

I particularly call your attention to the section of my resume headlined, Supervising print production atop page two.

I can make myself available for an interview at your convenience. Thank you for your time and consideration; I look forward to meeting you in the near future.

Cordially,

Jay Crago

ADVERTSING COORDINATOR
Career opportunity coordinating advertising for financial institution background in design, layout and copywriting required. Send resume to: Box AAA, NYT, New York, NY 10010.

88 Berkley Street
Maplewood, NJ 07040
201-555-9999

Dear Friends,

Certain magic words in your ad lead me to believe I may well be the perfect candidate for this opening, and I'm ready to make a real contribution.

Coordinating is a magic word to me because it's what I do best. Virtually all my previous positions have required a detail-oriented and successful organizer to pull everything together. Nowhere has this been more true than in my current position as a production manager in New York's largest ad agency.

Financial institution evokes satisfying memories of the work I did in my last position for the agency's client, Eastern Savings Bank. My work on that account was my most challenging and enjoyable. I became fascinated with the financial world, and I was adept at meeting the demands of the client, as the enclosed letter of recommendation from Stephen McMan will attest to.

Design, layout and copywriting are magic words because I have lots to contribute in those directions. My previous positions have always given me a certain involvement in design and layout, especially as editor of a city magazine in San Antonio, Texas. I have a keen interest and special education in the design and writing of company newsletters and other advertising pieces. I have lots of ideas for financial advertising.

Career opportunity is perhaps the most magic phrase of all as I have long been searching for a job I could really sink my teeth into for the long haul. This one seems so perfect because it combines my interest in the world of finance with my coordination talents and communications expertise.

I would be most happy to make myself available for an interview at your convenience.

Thanking you most kindly for your consideration of me, I look forward to hearing from you.

Sincerely,

Amy Marlowe

110 Appleton Court
Seattle, WA
98133206-555-4889

Dear Friends,

I have worn enough hats in the radio business to make me the "multi-talented" news director you're looking for. Now I'd like to contribute my energy and versatility to a leadership position in your organization.

My resume needs a bit of updating: I'm currently assistant news director of WGYB, one of the largest radio stations in Washington, dedicated to covering local and community news.

Here I've demonstrated superior management skills during the year as assistant news director, where I've been responsible for planning all news coverage and handing out assignments to a staff of 10 reporters and regional news directors. My excellent news judgment was recognized when I was promoted from regional news director to assistant news director after only three months at the station.

I have no qualms about my ability to produce innovative news programs in a competitive local market since the city market I'm currently in is one of the most competitive in the country, according to Arbitron.

The recent buyout of the station has left the future of the news staff uncertain, so I'm exploring new options. My supervisor, the news director of WGYB, will gladly attest to my superlative people-oriented skills and news judgment.

I currently make $24,000 a year, but my salary requirement is negotiable.

Thanking you most kindly for your consideration, I look forward to talking with you soon.

Sincerely,

Elizabeth C. Gretz

456 Palmetto Drive
Miami, FL 33154
305-555-4864

Mr. Peter O'Mally
Eastern Airlines
Miami International Airport
Miami, FL 33154

Dear Mr. O'Mally,

I'd like to thank you so much for taking the time—after hours—to
talk with me last Wednesday about career opportunities at
Eastern Airlines.

I was extremely impressed with how generous you were not only
with your time but with information. I learned a lot about the
airline business, a field I am very interested in entering but
about which I don't know as much as I should.

I also felt a warm rapport with you that I'm sure would lend
itself to an excellent working relationship. It's not just empty
flattery to tell you that my interview with you was one of the
best I've had during my current job search. You told me candidly
everything a potential employee would want to know about working
at Eastern. Your candor and willingness to offer information
makes me feel I would truly enjoy working for you.

As I told you at the interview, I think I have many talents that
could lend themselves to corporate relations—communications,
managerial and organizational skills, as well as creativity. I
believe my competent writing and broadcast experience could help
me make a meaningful contribution.

Mr. O'Mally, again, I thank you so much for your time and
interest. Thanks also for the letter you sent me last week. I
hope a spot develops ultimately that matches my talents because
I believe I could be quite happy and productive working for you.

Sincerely,

Amy D. Smith

Thank You Letter

- ○ Restates interest and enthusiasm for job
- ○ Compliments the company
- ○ Applicant expresses his understanding of job requirements
- ○ States willingness to come in for second interview
- ○ Possibly a bit too long
- ○ Grade: A-

4545 Easy Street
Portland, ME 04105
207-555-4554

Mr. Neal Anderson
U.S. Paper
120 Main Street
Portland, ME 04100

Dear Mr. Anderson,

I'd like to thank you for taking time to meet with me about timber management position you are creating.

I enjoyed meeting with you and got a good feeling about the level of professionalism at your company. I'm excited and intrigued by the possibility of assuming this position, especially because it is a new one.

I believe I could be a successful member of the Woodlands Department. At International Paper, I set up a timber management system that saved thousands of dollars in wasted timber.

I'm sure the experience I had managing the 10,000 acre division would be extremely helpful in the management of the timber in this new position.

My experience as a research technician of the United States Forest Fertilization Project has also given me a deep understanding of forest fertilization management, which could easily be applied to this position.

I believe I have a good understanding of the requirements of the position you are creating. I look forward to the possibility of coming on board to evaluate what you've been doing and looking for ways to do better.

Finally, I look forward to the possibility of working with you and Mr. O'Sullivan. Thank you again for meeting with me. I would very much like to make U.S. Paper known for having the most productive—at the lowest cost—timber lands in the country. If I can elaborate on my qualifications or answer any questions, I would be happy to come back for a second interview.

Sincerely,

Michael D. Jercko

83-59 189th Street
Bellerose, NY 11426
516-555-8359

Ms. Nancy Waller
AT&T
550 Madison Avenue
New York, NY 10022

Dear Ms. Waller,

I'd like to thank you for taking the time to talk with me Monday about the corporate adjuster position you have open at AT&T.

Your energetic presentation is enough to brighten anyone's Monday morning. I really appreciate that you would have taken so much time to acquaint me with the company and its benefits. That care shown to a potential employee makes me feel I would be very comfortable working there.

I also enjoyed the challenging, thoughtful talk I had with Mr. Ranch. I felt a rapport and respect for him that I feel would facilitate a good working relationship.

I feel I have a good understanding of the requirements of the position, and I am very interested. I am even more confident than before of my ability to make a real contribution to AT&T.

Ms. Waller, thanks again for talking with me Monday. Should you or Mr. Ranch want to talk with me further, I would be more than happy to oblige. I look forward to the possibility of working with you.

Cordially,

Anne P. Potter

Thank You Letter

- ○ Uses highlighting nicely to emphasize strengths of the interview
- ○ Provides an opportunity to send more information
- ○ Reiterates applicant's understanding of the next step in the process
- ○ Grade: A

233 K Street
Washington, D.C. 20520
202-555-4812

Dr. Jon Davidson
Director, University Relations
Georgetown University
Washington, D.C. 20007

Dear Dr. Davidson,

I'd like to thank you for taking the time to interview me for the staff writer position you have open.

I enjoyed meeting with you and am confident we could have an excellent working relationship.

Especially after meeting with you, I feel my background and expertise are a perfect fit for the job and its requirements.

Recapping my strengths and "fit" with the position:

— my previous short-term stints as staff writers with two suburban Washington colleges;

— my newspaper editing background would be an enormous asset because I have the inside track on what editors are looking for;

— my excellent "people skills" would enable me to fit into your congenial atmosphere as well as work well with the media and the university community;

I am also enclosing a piece I wrote expressing some of my ideas on how PR people could have more success getting their writing placed in the media.

Thank you again, Dr. Davidson, for your time and consideration. I look forward to hearing from you around the first of the year.

Sincerely yours,

Audrey M. Gleason

Recommended Reading

Obviously, cover letters make up a small—albeit important—part of the job-search process. Here are some books that can fill in the gaps if you're unfamiliar with how to mount a major job search.

What Color is Your Parachute (Richard Nelson Bolles, Ten Speed Press, $12.95.) The quintessential bible of job-hunting that, after almost twenty years, remains on lists of bestselling trade paperbacks and books most often checked out of libraries. This not a detailed guide to resumes, cover letters, interviewing techniques, and so on. It's a more basic volume directed at those who aren't quite sure what they want to be when they grow up, and those who've decided they want a new career. Updated every year, Parachute is loaded with exercises that help the jobseeker or career-changer gain self-knowledge needed to launch a successful job hunt. Bolles is not one to shy away from the more shocking statistics; he bombards the reader with reality because he wants to teach people how to tap the hidden job market. Enjoyable reading.

Who's Hiring Who (Richard Lathrop, Ten Speed Press, $9.95.) Something of a companion piece to Parachute. Bolles even calls it "the second best job-hunting guide on the market." Like Bolles, Lathrop emphasizes the hidden job market. Once you've read Bolles and know what you want to do, Lathrop will take you one step further, applying sharp marketing principles to resumes, cover letters, and interviews. Good information about interviewing, using contacts wisely, and getting maximum salary offers.

The Damn Good Resume Guide (Yana Parker, Ten Speed Press, $6.95.) A no-nonsense guide to resumes. Its format is extremely easy to follow, and it has many tips on creating effective resumes. It presents many samples of resumes and its companion volume, *The Resume Catalog* ($15.95), has even more.

Put Your Degree to Work (Marcia R. Fox, Norton, $6.95.) Particularly directed at soon-to-be college graduates, especially in professional fields. Teaches one how to act like a professional, make the best use of college placement services, and the importance of having a mentor. Decent chapters on resumes and cover letters, but the book really shines in the interview chapter.

Real World 101 (Calano and Salzman, Warner, $3.95.) Works well as a companion to Put Your Degree to Work. While the latter deals in the specifics of the job search, Real World 101 is more of a "head trip" book, designed to encourage students to adjust their attitudes to face life after college. The book spends relatively little time on job-hunting mechanics, more time talking about how college has failed you, making the most of the college time you have left, and developing professional style. Has a useful chapter on goal-setting, as well as one on developing the reading, writing, and listening skills so essential for success in the business world.

Jane Trahey on Women and Power (Jane Trahey, Avon, out of print but available at libraries.) A bit dated, but the very witty former advertising executive has a number of timeless tips to help women make it in a man's world. Like Parachute, it's a very enjoyable read.